Ohio's
Bicycle Trails

An American Bike Trails Publication

Ohio's
Bicycle Trails

Published by American Bike Trails

Copyright 2006 by American Bike Trails

Created by Ray Hoven

Illustrated & Designed by Mary C. Rumpsa

Table of Contents

How to Use this Book.. 6

Acknowledgements 6

Definition of Terms... 7

Definition of Terms (continued).. 8

Health Hazards... 10

Explanation of Symbols 12

Bicycle Safety... 13

Ohio Map 16

Trail Locations 18

Mileage between Principal Cities.. 20

Trails

Adena Recreational Trail 22

Alum Creek State Park 24

Barkcamp State Park 26

Beaver Creek State Park 28

Bike & Hike Trail 30

Blackhand Gorge Trail 32

Buckeye Trail.. 34

Caesar Creek State Park 36

Cleveland Lakefront State Park.. 39

Cleveland Metroparks 42

Big Creek Reservation 45

Mill Stream Run Reservation... 46

North Chagrin Reservation... 47

Ohio & Erie Canal Reservation 48

Rocky River Reservation.. 49

Conotton Creek Trail 50

Dillon State Park... 52

East Fork State Park.. 54

Findley State Park... 56

Gallipolis Bike Path 58

Gallia County Hike & Bike Trail 58

Great Ohio Lake-to-River Greenway 60

Western Reserve Greenway 60

Mill Creek Metroparks Bikeway (Canfield Rail-Trail) 60

Little Beaver Creek Greenway Trail 60

Table of Contents (continued)

Great Seal State Park 66

Harbin Park Mountain Bike Trail 68

Hockhocking Adena Bikeway 70

Holmes County Trail 72

Hueston Woods State Park 74

Huron River Greenway 76

Jefferson Lake State Park 78

John Bryan State Park 80

Kokosing Gap Trail 84

Lake Hope State Park 86

Lebanon Countryside Trail 88

Mary Jane Thurston State Park 90

Montgomery County's Trails 92

Great Miami River Recreation Trail 94

Wolf Creek Recreation Trail 96

Stillwater River Recreation Trail 98

Creekside Recreation Trail, Kettering Recreation Trail, Mad River Trail 100

North Coast Inland Trail 102

Oak Openings Preserve Metropark 106

Ohio to Erie Trail 108

Ohio & Erie Towpath 110

Heritage Rail-Trail 114

Licking County Recreation Trails 116

Thomas J. Evans Trail 116

Panhandle Trail 116

Prairie Grass Trail Xenia to South Charleston 119

Little Miami Scenic Trail 121

Olentangy-Scioto Bikeway 125

Paint Creek State Park 130

Pike State Forest 132

Richland B&O Trail 134

Scioto Trail State Forest 136

Shaker Trace Trail (Miami Whitewater Forest) 138

Simon Kenton Trail 140

Sippo Valley Trail 142

Slippery Elm Trail 146

Stavich Bicycle Trail 148
Stonelick State Park 150
University Parks Bike-Hike Trail 152
Van Buren State Park 154
Vulture's Knob 156
Race Course 156
Wabash Cannonball Trail 158
West Branch State Park 160
Black Creek Reservation 164
Buck Creek Trail 164
Celena to Coldwater Bike Trail 165
Greenway Corridor Bikeway 165
Hamilton Bikeway 165
Headwaters Trail 166
I-480 Bikeway 166
Lester Rail Trail 167
Lunken Airport Bike Path 167
National Road Bikeway 168
Nickelplate Trail 168
Oakwood Park 169
Piqua Linear Park 169
Westerville Bikeway 169
Wright Brothers Bikeway 170
Zanes Bikeway 170

Indexes
Organizations 171
Ohio Bicycle Clubs 172
Trail Index 177
Surfaced Trails 180
Mountain Bike Trails 182
City to Trail Index 183
County to Trail Index 187

How to Use this Book

This book provides a comprehensive, easy-to-use quick reference to many of the off-road trails throughout Ohio. Selections are generally limited to only ridable trails and trail sections 5 miles in length or more. Most trails are referenced in alphabetical sequence. Exceptions are those within Cleveland Metroparks, the Great Ohio Lake to River Greenway, Montgomery County's Trails, and the Ohio to Erie Trail system. Also included are sectional and trail location inset maps. Each trail map includes such helpful features as location and access, trail facilities, and nearby communities. In addition to a trail alphabetical index, the book also provides a cross-reference index by city to trail and by county to trail.

Acknowledgements

Karen Wells-Hamilton, MTBCHICK

Miami Valley Mountain Bike Association

Bob Feldman, Julie's Bike Shop Rentals

Cleveland Metroparks

Stark County Park District personnel

The many research contributions for this book from Ohio State Park & Forest personnel

Definition of Terms

Length   Expressed in miles one way. Round trip mileage is normally indicated for loops.

Effort Levels   **Easy** Physical exertion is not strenuous. Climbs and   descents as well as technical obstacles are more minimal. Recommended for beginners.

Moderate   Physical exertion is not excessive. Climbs and descents can be challenging. Expect some technical obstacles.

Difficult   Physical exertion is demanding. Climbs and descents require good riding skills. Trail surface may be sandy, loose rock, soft or wet.

Directions   Describes by way of directions and distances, how to get to the trail areas from roads and nearby communities.

Map   Illustrative representation of a geographic area, such as a state, section, forest, park or trail complex.

DNR   Department of Natural Resources

DOT   Department of Transportation

Explanation of Geological & Geographic Terms

Bog   An acidic wetland that is fed by rainwater and is characterized by open water with a floating mat of vegetation (e.g. sedges, mosses, tamarack) that will often bounce if you jump on it.

Bluff   A high steep bank with a broad, flat, or rounded front.

Canyon   A deep, narrow valley with precipitous sides, often with a stream flowing through it.

Drumlin   Smooth oval hill of glacial drift, elongated in the direction of the movement of the ice that deposited it. Drumlins may be more than 150 feet high and more than a half mile long.

Esker   A long winding, serpentine ridge of glacial drift (gravel) with steep sides (10-50 feet high).

Fen   An alkaline wetland that is fed by ground water and is often seen as a wet meadow and characterized by plants like Grass or Parnasis and sedges that grow in alkaline water.

7

Definition of Terms (continued)

Forest A vegetative community dominated by trees and many containing understory layers of smaller trees, shorter shrubs and an herbaceous layers at the ground.

Grove A small wooded area without underbrush, such as a picnic area.

Herb A seed producing annual, biennial, or perennial that does not develop persistent woody tissue but dies down at the end of a growing season.

Kame An oval depression of glacial till, often filled with water, formed when buried and stranded chunks of ice from a retreating glacier melted.

Kettle Oval depression found in glacial moraines, which are landforms made up of rock debris, which melts as the ground above it subsides, forming a kettle.

Lake A considerable inland body of standing water.

Marsh A wetland fed by streams and with shallow or deep water. Often characterized by mats of cattail, bulrushes, sedges and wetland forbs.

Mesic A type of plant that requires a moderate amount of water.

Moraine Long, irregular hills of glacial till deposited by stagnant and retreating glaciers.

Natural Community A group of living organisms that live in the same place, e.g. woodland or prairie.

Park An area maintained in its natural state as a public property.

Pond A body of water usually smaller than a lake.

Prairie Primarily treeless grassland community characterized by full sun and dominated by perennial, native grasses and forbs.

Preserve An area restricted for the protection and preservation of natural resources.

Ridge A range of hills or mountains.

Savanna	A grassland ecosystem with scattered trees characterized by native grasses and forbs.
Sedges	Grass-like plants with triangular stems and without showy flowers. Many are dominant in sedge meadows, bogs and fens but others are found in woodlands or prairies.
Shrubs	Low woody plants, usually shorter than trees and with several stems.
Swale	A lower lying or depressed and off wet stretch of land.
Swamp	Spongy land saturated and sometimes partially or intermittently covered with water.
Turf	The upper stratum of soil bound by grass and plant roots into a thick mat.
Wetland	The low lying wet area between higher ridges.

Health Hazards

Hypothermia

Hypothermia is a condition where the core body temperature falls below 90 degrees. This may cause death.

Mild hypothermia

1. Symptoms	a.	Pronounced shivering
	b.	Loss of physical coordination
	c.	Thinking becomes cloudy
2. Causes	a.	Cold, wet, loss of body heat, wind
3. Treatment	a.	Prevent further heat loss, get out of wet clothing and out of wind. Replace wet clothing with dry.
	b.	Help body generate more heat. Refuel with high-energy foods and a hot drink, get moving around, light exercise, or external heat.

Severe hypothermia

1. Symptoms	a.	Shivering stops, pulse and respiration slows down, speech becomes incoherent.
2. Treatment	a.	Get help immediately.
	b.	Don't give food or water.
	c.	Don't try to rewarm the victim in the field.
	d.	A buildup of toxic wastes and tactic acid accumulates in the blood in the body's extremities. Movement or rough handling will cause a flow of the blood from the extremities to the heart. This polluted blood can send the heart into ventricular fibrillations (heart attack), and may result in death.
	e.	Wrap victim in several sleeping bags and insulate from the ground.

Frostbite

Symptoms of frostbite may include red skin with white blotches due to lack of circulation. Rewarm body parts gently. Do not immerse in hot water or rub to restore circulation, as both will destroy skin cell.

Heat Exhaustion

Cool, pale, and moist skin, heavy sweating, headache, nausea, dizziness and vomiting. Body temperature nearly normal.

Treatment — Have victim lie in the coolest place available–on back with feet raised. Rub body gently with cool, wet cloth. Give person ½ glass of water every 15 minutes if conscious and can tolerate it. Call for emergency medical assistance.

Heat Stroke

Hot, red skin, shock or unconsciousness; high body temperature.

Treatment — Treat as a life-threatening emergency. Call for emergency medical assistance immediately. Cool victim by any means possible. Cool bath, pour cool water over body, or wrap wet sheets around body. Give nothing by mouth.

West Nile Virus

West Nile Virus is transmitted by certain types of mosquitoes. Most people infected with West Nile Virus won't develop symptoms. Some may become ill 3 to 15 days after being bitten.

Protect Yourself — Wear proper clothing, use insect repellents and time your outdoor activities to reduce your risk of mosquito bites and other insect problems. Most backyard mosquito problems are caused by mosquitoes breeding in and around homes, not those from more natural areas.

Explanation of Symbols

SYMBOL LEGEND

- 🏊 Beach/Swimming
- 🚲 Bicycle Repair
- 🏠 Cabin
- ▲ Camping
- 🛶 Canoe Launch
- ➕ First Aid
- 🍴 Food
- GC Golf Course
- ? Information
- 🛏 Lodging
- MF Multi-Facilities
- P Parking
- 🏔 Picnic
- 🚶 Ranger Station
- 🚻 Restrooms
- 🏠 Shelter
- T Trailhead
- 🏛 Visitor Center
- 🚰 Water
- 🔭 Overlook/ Observation

AREA LEGEND

- City, Town
- Parks, Preserves
- Waterway
- Marsh/Wetland
- ▬▬ Mileage Scale
- ★ Points of Interest
- – – County/State
- 🌲 Forest/Woods

TRAIL LEGEND

- ▬▬▬▬ Trail-Biking/Multi
- ·············· Hiking only Trail
- •••••••••• Hiking - Multi Use
- ▬▬▬▬ Snowmobiling only
- ========= Planned Trail
- ▬ ▬ ▬ ▬ Alternate Trail
- ▬▬▬▬ Road/Highway
- +++++++++++ Railroad Tracks

Bicycle Safety

Bicycling offers many rewards, among them a physically fit body and a pleasant means of transportation. But the sport has its hazards, which can lead to serious accidents and injuries. We have provided rules, facts and tips that can help minimize the dangers of bicycling while you're having fun.

Choose The Right Bicycle

Adults and children should ride bicycles with frames small enough to be straddled easily with both feet flat on the ground, and with handlebars that can be easily reached with elbows bent. Oversize bikes make it difficult to ride comfortably and maintain control. Likewise, don't buy a large bike for a child to grow into--smaller is safer.

Learn To Ride The Safe Way

When learning to ride a bike, let a little air out of the tires, and practice steering and balancing by "scootering" around with both feet on the ground and the seat as low as possible. The "fly-or-fall" method-where someone runs alongside the bicycle and then lets go-can result in injuries.

Training wheels don't work, since the rider can't learn to balance until the wheels come of. They can be used with a timid rider, but the child still will have to learn to ride without them. Once the rider can balance and pedal (without training wheels), raise the seat so that the rider's leg is almost straight at the bottom of the pedal stroke.

Children seldom appreciate the dangers and hazards of city cycling. Make sure they understand the traffic laws before letting them onto the road.

Use This Important Equipment

A working headlight and rear reflector are required for night riding in some states. Side reflectors do not make the rider visible to drivers on cross streets.

Safety seat for children under 40 lbs. Make sure the seat is mounted firmly over the rear wheel of the bike, and does not wobble when going downhill at high speed. Make sure the child will not slide down while riding. The carrier should also have a device to keep the child's feet from getting into the spokes.

Package Racks are inexpensive, and they let the rider steer with both hands and keep packages out of the spokes.

Bicycle Safety (continued)

Beware Of Dangerous Practices

Never ride against traffic. Failure to observe this rule causes the majority of car-bicycle collisions. Motorists can't always avoid the maneuvers of a wrong-way rider since the car and bike move toward each other very quickly.

Never make a left turn from the right lane.

Never pass through an intersection at full speed.

Never ignore stop light or stop signs.

Never enter traffic suddenly from a driveway or sidewalk. This rule is particularly important when the rider is a child, who is more difficult for a motorist to see.

Don't wear headphones that make it hard to hear and quickly respond to traffic.

Don't carry passengers on a bike. The only exception is a child under 40 lbs. who is buckled into an approved bike safety seat and wears a helmet as required by law.

Passenger trailers can be safe and fun. Be aware, though, that a trailer makes the bike much longer and requires careful control. Passengers must wear helmets.

Get A Bike That Works With You

Skilled riders who use their bikes often for exercise or transport should consider buying multi-geared bikes, which increase efficiency while minimizing stress on the body. (These bikes may not be appropriate for young or unskilled riders, who may concentrate more on the gears than on the road.) The goal is to keep the pedals turning at a rate of 60-90 RPM. Using the higher gears while pedaling slowly is hard on the knees, and is slower and more tiring than the efficient pedaling on the experienced cyclist. Have a safe trip!

Emergency Toolkit

When venturing out on bicycle tours, it is always smart to take along equipment to help make roadside adjustments and repairs. It is not necessary for every member of your group to carry a complete set of equipment, but make sure someone in your group brings along the equipment listed below:

1.) Standard or slotted screwdriver
2.) Phillips screwdriver
3.) 6" or 8" adjustable wrench
4.) Small pliers
5.) Spoke adjuster
6.) Tire pressure gauge
7.) Portable tire pump
8.) Spare innertube
9.) Tire-changing lugs

A Few Other Things

When embarking on a extended bike ride, it is important to give your bike a pre-ride check. To ensure that your bike is in premium condition, go over the bike's mechanisms, checking for any mechanical problems. It's best to catch these at home, and not when they occur "on the road." If you run into a problem that you can't fix yourself, you should check your local yellow pages for a professional bike mechanic.

When you are planning a longer trip, be sure to consider your own abilities and limitations, as well as those of any companions who may be riding with you. In general, you can ride about three times the length (time-wise) as your average training ride. If you have a regular cycling routine, this is a good basis by which to figure the maximum distance you can handle.

Finally, be aware of the weather. Bring plenty of sunblock for clear days, and rain gear for the rainy one. Rain can make some rides miserable, in addition to making it difficult to hear other traffic. Winds can blow up sand, and greatly increase the difficulty of a trail.

Trail Courtesy & Common Sense

1.) Stay on designated trails.
2.) Bicyclists use the right side of the trail (Walkers use the left side of the trail).
3.) Bicyclists should only pass slower users on the left side of the trail; use your voice to warn others when you need to pass.
4.) Get off to the side of the trail if you need to stop.
5.) Bicyclists should yield to all other users.
6.) Do not use alcohol or drugs while on the trail.
7.) Do not litter.
8.) Do not trespass onto adjacent land.
9.) Do not wear headphones while using the trail.

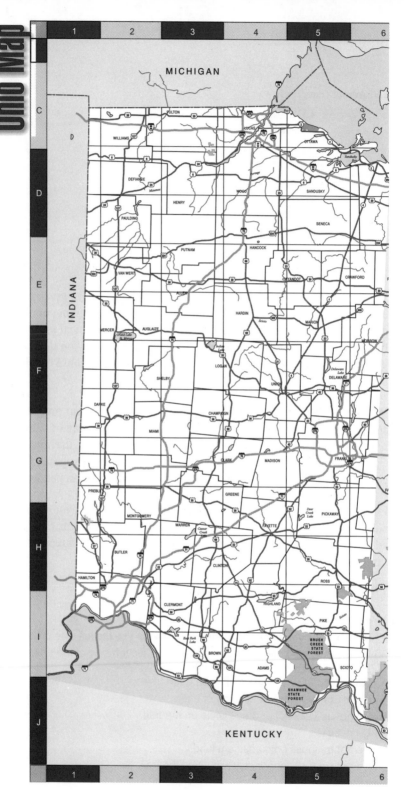

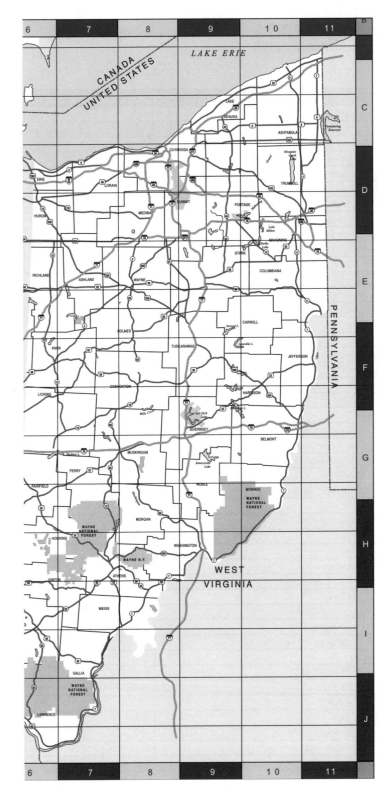

Trail Locations

Trail Name	Map Location	Bk Pg
Adena Recreation Trail	H 5	22
Alum Creek State Park	F 5	24
Barkcamp State Park	G10	26
Beaver Creek State Park	E11	28
Bedford Reservation	D 9	42
Big Creek Reservation	D 8	44
Bike and Hike Trail	D 9	30
Black River Reservation	C 7	164
Blackhand Gorge Bikeway	G 7	32
Brecksville Reservation	D 8	42
Buck Creek Trail	G 4	164
Caesar Creek State Park	H 3	36
Celina to Coldwater Bike Trail	F 2	165
Cleveland Lakefront State Park	C 8-9	39
Conotton Creek Trail	F10	50
Creekside Trail	G 3	100
Dillon State Park	G 8	52
East Fork State Park	I 3	54
Euclid Creek Reservation	D 8	42
Findley State Park	D 7	56
Gallipolis Bike Path	I 7	58
Garfield Park Reservation	C 9	42
Great Miami River Recreation Trail	G 3	94
Great Ohio Lake to River Greenway	C10	60
Great Seal State Park	H 5	66
Greenway Corridor Bikeway	C 9	165
Hamilton Bikeway	H 2	165
Harbin Park Mountain Bike Trail	H 2	68
Headwaters Trail	D 9	166
Heritage Rail-Trail	G 5	114
Hinckley Reservation	D 8	43
Hockhocking-Adena Bikeway	H 7	70
Holmes County Trail	EF8	72
Hueston Woods State Park	H 1	74
Huntington Reservation	D 8	43
Huron River Greenway	D 6	76
I-480 Bikepath	D 8	166
Jefferson Lake State Park	F10	78
John Bryan State Park	G 4	80
Kettering Recreation Trail	G 3	100
Kokosing Gap Trail	F 7	84
Lake Hope State Park	H 7	86
Lebanon Countryside Trail	H 2	88
Lester Trail	D 8	167

Trail Name	Map Location	Bk Pg
Licking County Recreation Trails	G 6	116
Little Beaver Creek Greenway Trail	E10	62
Little Miami Scenic Trail	GH4	121
Lunken Airport Bike Path	I 2	167
Mad River Recreation Trail	G 3	100
Mary Jane Thurston State Park	D 3	90
Mill Creek Metroparks Bikeway	E10	61
Mill Stream Run Reservation	D 8	45
National Road Bikeway	G10	168
Nickelplate Trail	E 9	168
North Chagrin Reservation	C 9	46
North Coast Inland Trail	D 4-5	102
Oak Openings Preserve Metropark	C 3	106
Oakwood Park	D 3	169
Ohio & Erie Canal Reservation	D 8	47
Ohio & Erie Towpath Trail	DE9	110
Ohio to Erie Trail	DH3-8	108
Olentangy-Scioto Bikeway	G 5	125
Paint Creek State Park	H 4	130
Panhandle Trail	G 7	116
Pike State Forest	I 5	132
Piqua Linear Park	F 2	169
Prairie Grass Trail	G 3-4	119
Richland B&O Trail	E 6	134
Rocky River Reservation	D 8	48
Scioto Trail State Forest & Park	I 5	136
Shaker Trail	I 2	138
Simon Kenton Trail	G 4	140
Sippo Valley Trail	E 9	142
Slippery Elm Trail	D 4	146
South Chagrin Reservation	D 9	43
Stavich Bicycle Trail	D11	148
Stillwater River Recreation Trail	G 2	98
Stonelick State Park	I 3	150
Thomas J Evans Trail	G 6	116
University Parks Bike-Hike Trail	C 4	152
Van Buren State Park	D 4	154
Vulture's Knob	E 8	156
Wabash Cannonball Trail	C 2-4	158
West Branch State Park	D10	160
Western Reserve Greenway	CE10	61
Westerville Bikeway	G 5	169
Wolf Creek Recreation Trail	G 2	96
Wright Brothers Bikeway	G 3	170
Zanes Bikeway	G 7	170

Mileage between Principal Cities

CITIES	1	2	3	4	5	6	7	8	9	10	11	12	13	14
1 Akron		24	173	236	34	127	198	120	102	83	171	129	35	49
2 Canton	24		172	235	58	126	197	132	101	99	170	141	31	53
3 Chillicothe	173	172		90	185	46	76	142	92	152	68	187	141	220
4 Cincinnati	236	235	90		248	109	55	163	145	215	82	208	204	283
5 Cleveland	34	58	185	248		139	210	117	114	64	183	110	57	66
6 Columbus	127	126	46	109	139		71	96	46	106	44	141	95	174
7 Dayton	198	197	76	55	210	71		108	90	154	27	153	166	245
8 Findlay	120	132	142	163	117	96	108		50	131	75	172	93	185
9 Marion	102	101	92	145	114	46	90	50		64	63	95	70	149
10 Sandusky	83	99	152	215	64	106	154	131	64		127	54	68	122
11 Springfield	171	170	68	82	183	44	27	75	63	127		130	139	218
12 Toledo	129	141	187	208	110	141	153	172	95	54	130		110	168
13 Wooster	35	31	141	204	57	95	166	93	70	68	139	110		83
14 Youngstown	49	53	220	283	66	174	245	185	149	122	218	168	83	

Trails

Adena Recreational Trail

Trail Uses	 (icons)
Area	Chillicothe
Trail Length	7 miles
Surface	Asphalt

Trail Notes

The Adena Recreational Trail will eventually link Chillicothe to Washington Court House for a length of more than 30 miles. It will travel almost entirely on the abandoned B&O Railroad corridor. From Washington Court House the trail will continue through Jamestown to Xenia where it will line up with the Ohio to Erie cross state trail.

Currently the trail begins near the Maple Grove/Anderson Station/ Sulphur Lick Roads intersection. The first section travels through the site of a Hopewell Indian village. It then travels toward the Village of Frankfort crossing five bridges. The longest bridge, some three miles from Frankfort, is 266 feet long and provides a scenic overlook as it crosses the North Fork of Paint Creek.

Parking is available at the Hopewell Site, and in Mantua, Hiram Station and Garrettsville.

Getting There

From Cincinnati, take Route 28 east to Chillicothe. From Columbus, take Hwy 23 south to Chillicothe.

Contact

Ross County Park District   740-774-8794
15 North Paint Street
Chillicothe, Ohio 45601

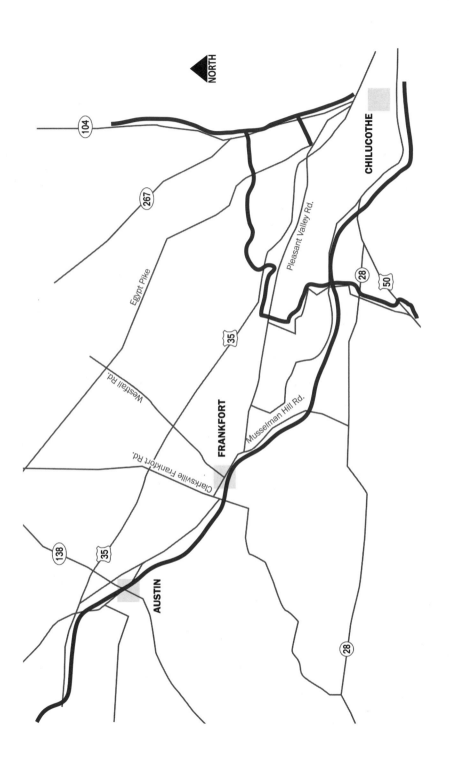

Alum Creek State Park

Trail Uses   🚴 🚵 🏃 🚶 ⛷

Area	Columbus
Trail Length	13 miles
Surface	Natural

Trail Notes

Located less than 10 miles north of Columbus, Alum Creek's 3,387 acre reservoir and gently rolling span of fields and woodlands provide a hub of recreational activity. The trails wind along the lakeshore through mature beech-maple forests and across deep ravines. Water and latrines are available. Alum Creek resides in the midst of the fertile agricultural till plains and river valleys of Delaware County. The park offers a diverse array of natural features. Cliffs of Ohio shale are notable in many areas, exposed as Alum Creek and other streams cut through underlying bedrock. The dark hue of the rock is due to the carbonized plant material and mud that formed the shale.

In October of 2005, Phase II mountain biking was opened in a ceremony held in conjunction with the Central Ohio Mountain Biking Organization (COMBO) and Alum Creek State Park. It was hand built by COMBO through its volunteer labor, and added about 6 miles of singletrack trail. See the trail map inset for an illustration of Phase II.

In addition to mountain biking there are many miles of trails available for horseback riding and snowmobiling. Other facilities include campsites, equipped Rent-A-RV units, picnicking, boating, a 3,000 foot swimming beach, and concessions.

Getting There

Alum Creek State Park is located in Delaware County just north of Columbus, west of I-71 and east of State Route 23. Access points include Africa Road, Hollenback Road, Peachblow Road, Cheshire Road, Hwy 36, and several more.

Contact

Alum Creek State Park   740-548-4631
3615 S. Old State Road
Delaware, OH 43015
Camping & Rentals   866-644-6727

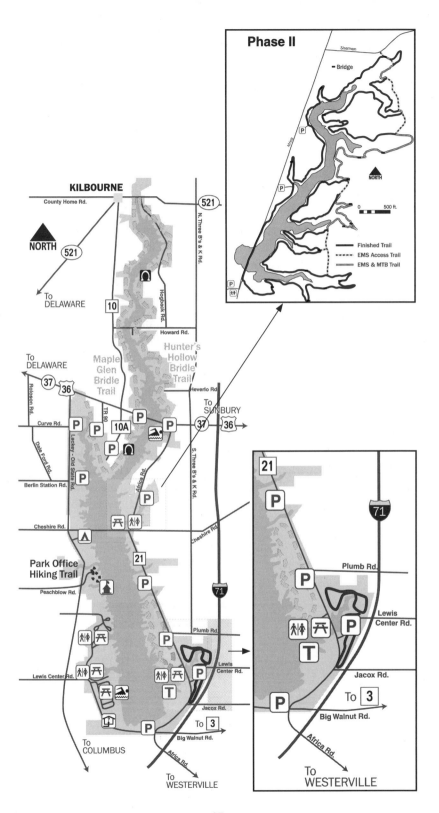

Barkcamp State Park

Trail Uses	🚴 🚶 🎧 ⛰️
Area	Clairsville & Barnesville
Trail Length	6 miles
Surface	Natural

Trail Notes

The mountain bike trail system was built and is currently maintained by volunteers. While there is no illustrated map detailing these trails at present, they were built within the Lakeview & Woodland Trail hiking loops. See below for directions.

Barkcamp State Park is a setting of rugged hills, mature woodlands, open meadows, a scenic lake, abundant wildlife, and some great recreational facilities. The electrified campsites feature hot showers, tables and a dump station. There are three Rent-A-Camp units available for reservation and two deluxe Camper Cabins. The sandstone hills of the Barkcamp region are part of the Appalachian highlands, which envelop the southeastern part of Ohio.

Getting There

From I-70, take SR 149 south to TR 92. Go east of TR 92 to the park entrance. Take the park road east, crossing the lake twice to a parking area on your left. Cross the road and follow the path to the Lakeview Hiking Trail where you will find entrances to the mountain bike trails.

Contact

Barkcamp State Park   740-484-4064
65330 Barkcamp Park Road
Belmont, Ohio 43715

TRAIL LEGEND	
———————	Trail-Biking/Multi
··············	Hiking only Trail
••••••••••	Hiking - Multi Use
▀▄▀▄▀▄▀	Snowmobiling only
=========	Planned Trail
▬ ▬ ▬ ▬ ▬	Alternate Trail
———————	Road/Highway
┼┼┼┼┼┼┼┼┼	Railroad Tracks

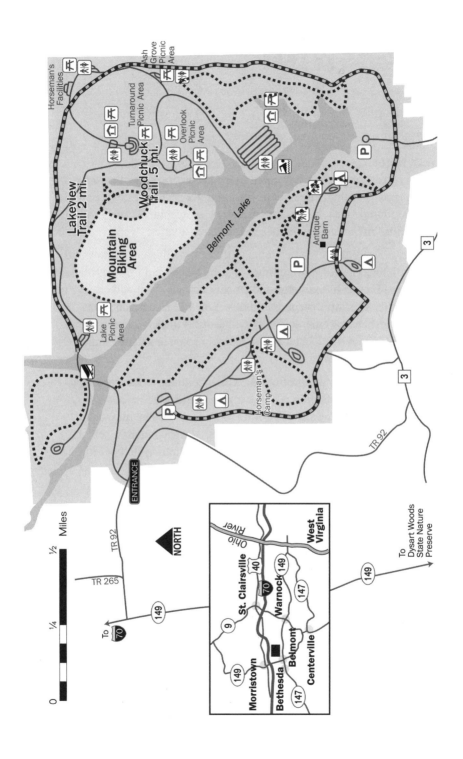

Horseman's Facilities

Ash Grove Picnic Area

Turnaround Picnic Area

Overlook Picnic Area

Lakeview Trail 2 mi.

Woodchuck Trail .5 mi.

Mountain Biking Area

Lake Picnic Area

Belmont Lake

Antique Barn

Horseman's Camp

ENTRANCE

P

3

3

TR 92

TR 92

TR 265

To 70

Miles

0   ¼   ½

NORTH

Ohio River

St. Clairsville

West Virginia

Warnock

Belmont

Centerville

Bethesda

Morristown

9

40

70

149

149

149

147

147

149

To Dysart Woods State Nature Preserve

Beaver Creek State Park

Trail Uses	🚵 🥾 🎿
Area	Cleveland
Trail Length	9 miles
Surface	Natural, groomed

Trail Notes

Beaver Creek State Park is located in the sandstone hills of eastern Ohio. There are two technical mountain biking trails – Vondergreen, and the Dogwood trail. They both offer great scenery, technical climbs, and fun downhills, but are not recommended for the beginner.

Vondergreen is about 7 miles long, with some rolling singletrack and steep climbs. There are two entrances – the Upper and Lower. Head up the road to get to the suggested Upper entrance. You will cross bridle trails for short distances at times. You will also come across to the Gretchen and Grey locks. It's a beautiful track without a lot of switchbacks, but it is technical and rocky in some areas plus some very fast sections.

Dogwood is directly across from the entrance to the Vondergreen, at the end of the road. Facilities at the trailhead include restrooms and picnic tables. Dogwood is a two mile loop, with the first mile being easy singletrack with some twist and turns. The second mile gets more technical and hilly, with one near impossible climb. Watch out for the ravines. You may even want to hike the last quarter mile.

Getting There

From East Liverpool, take Hwy 30/SR 11 North to SR 170, then continue north on SR 170 past the small town of Calcutta to CR 428 (Sprucevale Road). About 4 miles north on CR 428 you'll come to a junction. Proceed left, then south into the park to a parking area near the Pioneer Village. You can access the southern trailhead of Vondergreen Trail via the park entrance shortly after you pass over Little Beaver Creek on CR 428.

Contact

Beaver Creek State Park 330-385-3091
12021 Echo Dell Road
East Liverpool, Ohio 43920

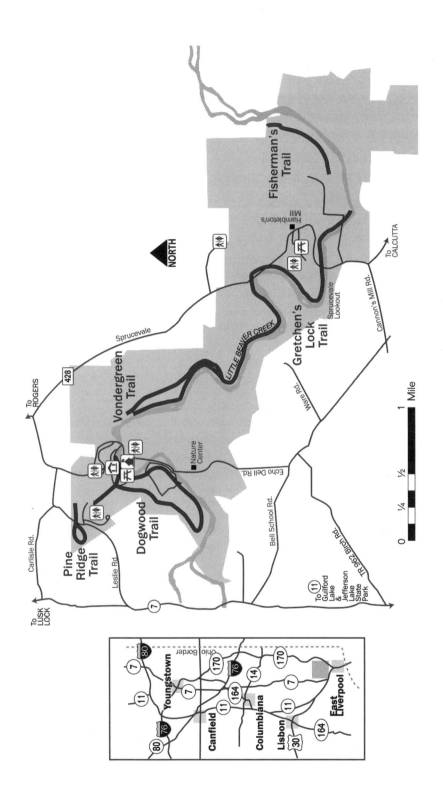

NORTH

To ROGERS

428

Sprucevale

Vondergreen Trail

LITTLE BEAVER CREEK

Gretchen's Lock Trail

Sprucevale Lookout

Hambleton's Mill

Fisherman's Trail

To CALCUTTA

Cannon's Mill Rd.

Wate Rd.

Echo Dell Rd.

Nature Center

Bell School Rd.

TR 962 Birch Rd.

To (11)
Guilford
Lake
&
Jefferson
Lake
State
Park

Dogwood Trail

Pine Ridge Trail

Leslie Rd

Carlisle Rd.

To LUSK LOCK

7

0   ¼   ½   1   Mile

Ohio Border

80

7

11

7

170

76

14

170

7

164

11

Youngstown

Canfield

Columbiana

Lisbon

30

164

11

East Liverpool

164

76

80

Bike & Hike Trail

Trail Uses	🚴 🎿 🏃
Area	Summit County – Brandywine Falls to Munroe Falls
Trail Length	33.5 miles
Surface	Asphalt, crushed gravel

Trail Notes

The 33.5 mile Trail was one of the first rails-to-trail conversions in the country. It follows the course of the old Akron, Bedford & Cleveland (ABC) Railroad, which was the longest electric railroad of its kind when built in 1895. East of Route 91 in Munroe Falls, the Bike & Hike Trail parallels a scenic section of the Cuyahoga River where numerous waterfowl can be seen. South of Boston Mills Road in Boston Heights, the Sharon Conglomerate rock wall of the Boston Leges rises along the trail. Farther north, the trail travels along Brandywine Road. There is a parking area adjacent to the bridge over I-271, which offers rest and a view of Brandywine Falls, one of the highest waterfalls in Ohio at 75 feet.

The Bike & Hike Trail is surfaced with asphalt or compacted limestone. Except for the unpaved section in Stow between Hudson Drive and Young Road, the trail is suitable for rollerblading. Some portions of the trail use neighborhood streets. The trail is mostly flat and smooth, and many of the street crossings provide signs with street names and distances to the next street.

Restrooms are located at the SR 303, Springdale, Silver Springs Park and SR 91 lots. There is a volunteer Bike Patrol to assist visitors and provide staff with up-to-date information on trail conditions.

Contact

Summit County Metro Park
330-867-5511
975 Treaty Lane Road
Akron, OH 44313

TRAIL LEGEND	
▬▬▬▬	Trail-Biking/Multi
··············	Hiking only Trail
••••••••••	Hiking - Multi Use
▰▰▰▰▰▰	Snowmobiling only
==========	Planned Trail
▬ ▬ ▬ ▬ ▬	Alternate Trail
▬▬▬▬	Road/Highway
++++++++++	Railroad Tracks

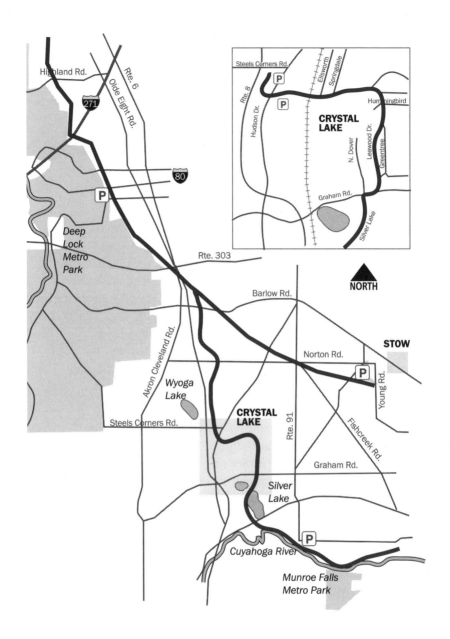

Access Locations

SR 82 lots	685 & 686 Aurora Road, Sagamore Hills
Brandywine Falls	8514 Brandywine Road, Northfield Center
Boston Heights	298 Boston Mills Road W., Boston Heights
SR303 lot	64 W. Streetsboro Road, Boston Heights
Barlow lot	331 Barlow Road, Hudson
Springdale lot	968 Springdale Road, Stow
Silver Lake Town Hall	2985 Kent Road, Stow
SR91 lot	130 N. Main Street, Munroe Falls
Silver Springs Park	5027 Stow Road, Stow

Blackhand Gorge Trail

Trail Uses   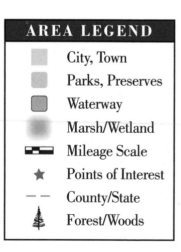

Area	Hanover
Trail Length	4.3 miles
Surface	Asphalt

Trail Notes

The trail follows the Licking River on the its south side from the main parking lot to the west parking lot in Blackhand Gorge State Nature Preserve. The prime feature of this 956 acre preserve is the east-west gorge cut by the Licking River through the Black Hand sandstone formation. The hilltops are dominated by oak, hickory, Virginia pine and mountain laurel, with mixed hardwoods and spring flora on the wooded slopes and ravines. By 1929 the gorge had witnessed the passing of the canal boats, trolley and steam locomotives, but the remains of the old canal lock still dot the preserve. The preserve is open all year, from daylight to dusk.

Getting There

Take Marne Road east at Licking Valley Road from the Panhandle. Where the road shortly rounds a bend, bear right to cross Route 16, which becomes Brownsville Road. Cross Route 16 and turn left on Brushy Ford Road. The small, unmarked parking area will come up on your left and is the west end of the Blackhand Trail. Total connection distance is 1.2 miles.

Contact

Division of Natural Areas and Preserves
740-763-4411
2045 Morse Road
Columbus, Bldg. F-1, OH 43229

AREA LEGEND	
	City, Town
	Parks, Preserves
	Waterway
	Marsh/Wetland
▄▄	Mileage Scale
★	Points of Interest
– –	County/State
🌲	Forest/Woods

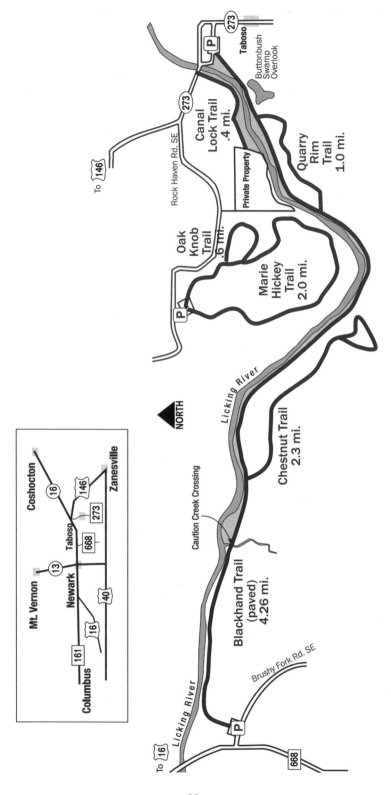

273

Taboso

Buttonbush
Swamp
Overlook

273

Canal
Lock Trail
.4 mi.

To 146

Rock Haven Rd. SE

Private Property

Quarry
Rim
Trail
1.0 mi.

Oak
Knob
Trail
.6 mi.

Marie
Hickey
Trail
2.0 mi.

Licking River

NORTH

Chestnut Trail
2.3 mi.

Caution Creek Crossing

Blackhand Trail
(paved)
4.26 mi.

Brushy Fork Rd. SE

To 16

Licking River

668

Coshocton

16

Zanesville

146

273

Taboso

668

Mt. Vernon

13

Newark

40

161

16

Columbus

Buckeye Trail

Area	State of Ohio
Trail Length	1,435 miles
Surface	Mixed

Trail Notes

The nearly 1,435 miles making up the Buckeye Trail wind around Ohio reaching into every corner of the state. This trail system was first envisioned in the late 1950's as a trail from the Ohio River to Lake Erie, but evolved into a large loop. Although conceived as a hiking trail, many sections are designated trails open to biking and are referenced in this book. As a statewide trail it follows old canal towpaths, abandoned railroad rights of way, rivers, lakeshores, rural by ways and primitive footpaths over forest public and private lands. The Buckeye Trail traverses over 40 of Ohio's 88 counties, passing through forests, state and local parks, many small towns and urban areas.

The trail is identified by blue blazes. These are the 2" by 6" vertical blue makings painted on trees and utility poles every few hundred feet along the trail. Where the trail changes directions it is marked with double blazes with the upper blaze offset in the new direction. A double blaze with no offset simply means the trail route may not be obvious. Camping is permitted at designated campsites, but may not be frequent enough to camp beside the trail every night, especially for backpackers. The trail is maintained and managed by the Buckeye Trail Association, a private, non-profit organization.

Contact

Buckeye Trail Association   800-881-3082
P.O. Box 254, Worthington, OH 43085
www.buckeyetrail.org

There are 26 sections to the Buckeye Trail,
each named for a town or feature within the
section, and each with its experiences.

1	Akron	14	Norwalk
2	Bedford	15	Old Man's
3	Belle Valley		Cave
4	Bowerston	16	Pemberville
5	Burton	17	Road Fork
6	Caesar	18	St. Marys
	Creek	19	Scioto Trail
7	Defiance	20	Shawnee
8	Delphos	21	Sinking
9	Loveland		Spring
10	Massillon	22	Stockport
11	Medina	23	Troy West
12	Mogador		Union
13	New	24	Whipple
	Straitsville	25	Williamsburg

Caesar Creek State Park

Trail Uses	🚲 🏃 🎿 🧗
Area	Cincinnati, Dayton
Trail Length	18 miles
Surface	Natural

Trail Notes

The centerpiece of Caesar Creek State Park is Caesar Creek Lake, a flood control and recreation reservoir created by the U.S. Army Corps of Engineers. The lake covers 2,830 acres and is over 8 miles long. The setting includes clear blue waters, scattered woodlands, meadows and steep ravines.

There are 4 trails in the park's mountain biking trail system. The Harveysburg loop, at a little over 5 miles, is located near the north end of Harveysburg Road and is marked with red caps on PCV posts. The Campground loop, at about 2.5 miles, is located at the top of the map inset and is marked with green caps on PCV posts. The Ward Road trailhead is located in the center of the map inset. The loop is 5.5 miles long and is identified with blue caps on PCV posts. The Turkey Run loop is 4.3 miles long, and connects the green and blue loops. It is marked with yellow caps on PVC posts. The Brimstone trailhead is located in the lower right of the map inset. These trails are maintained by the Cincinnati Off Road Alliance (CORA).

In addition to mountain biking there are 43 miles of hiking trails, 31 miles of bridle trails, snowmobiling and cross-country skiing. There is a 1,300 foot beach with changing booths and a concession area. Electrified campsites include flush toilets, hot showers, and dump stations.

Getting There

From Columbus, take I-71 South to State Route 73. West on SR73 to Harveysburg Road, then north about a mile to a parking area near the south trailhead of the mountain bike trail.

From Cincinnati, take I-71 North to State Route 73. West on SR 73 to Harversburg Road as described above.

From Xenia, take US 42 south to Waynesville and the State Route 73 intersection. East on SR73 to Harveysburg Road, then north to the south trailhead and parking.

Contact

Caesar Creek State Park 513-897-3055
8570 East S.R. 73
Waynesville, OH 45068

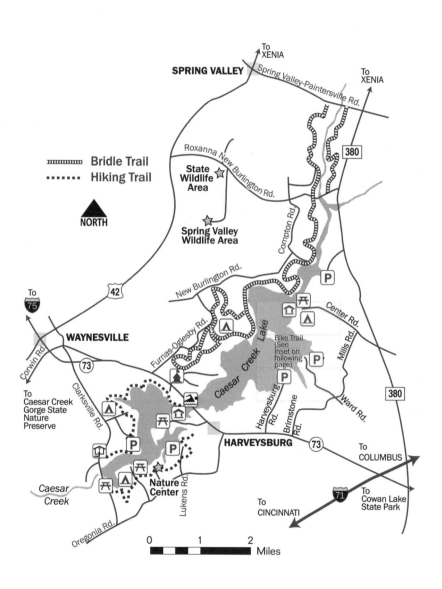

Caesar Creek State Park (continued)

Mountain Biking Trails

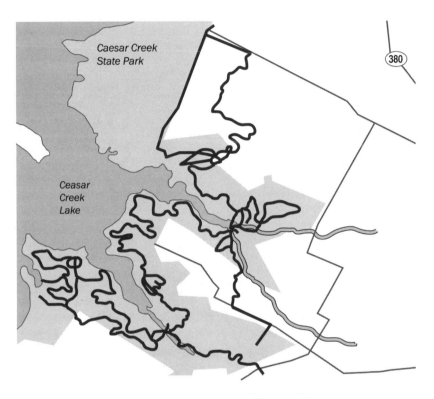

Overview

Cleveland Lakefront State Park

Trail Uses

Area   Cleveland

Trail Length   9 miles

Surface   Paved

Trail Notes

The Cleveland Lakefront State Park is divided into upper and lower areas connected by a paved bicycle path and fitness course. Upper Edgewater has restroom facilities and is within walking distance of the 900 foot swimming beach. Lower Edgewater features a swimming beach, restrooms and a concession facility.

The 9 mile bike trail traces the Lake Erie shoreline along Cleveland's Lakeshore Boulevard from East 9th Street to East 185th Street. The route provides access to the East 55th Street Marina, Gordon Park, Euclid Beach, Villa Angela and Wildwood Park areas. The is also a quarter mile bike path linking East 55th Street Marina and Gordon Park, and a 1 mile bike path connecting Euclid Beach and Villa Angela, with a half mile spur to Wildwood.

Area Attractions

*Headlands Beach State Park is located east of Cleveland near Fairport Harbor, and is the longest natural sand beach in Ohio.

*Headlands Dunes, the adjacent state nature preserve, is one of the finest examples of the Lake's beach and dune communities remaining in Ohio, with rare plant species normally found only on the Atlantic coast.

*Mentor Marsh State Nature Preserve, just south of Headlands Beach, is a 644 acre marsh-swamp forest containing unique plant and animal life.

*Hach-Otis State Nature Preserve, located east of Cleveland off SR174, is a remnant mature forest in the Chagrin River Valley.

*Punderson State Park, located in Geauga County, is a resort park offering a campground, lodging, winter recreation area, and golf course.

Contact

Cleveland Lakefront State Park   216-881-8141
8701 Lakeshore Blvd., N.E.
Cleveland, Ohio 44108

Cleveland Lakefront State Park (continued)

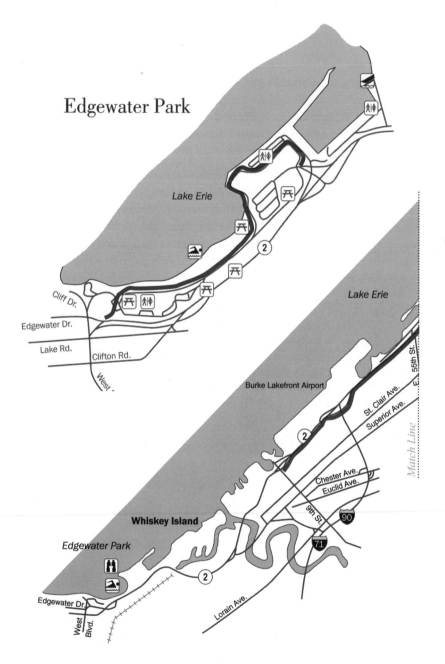

Edgewater Park

Lake Erie

Lake Erie

Cliff Dr.

Edgewater Dr.

Lake Rd.

Clifton Rd.

West

Burke Lakefront Airport

St. Clair Ave.

Superior Ave.

E. 55th St.

Match Line

Chester Ave.

Euclid Ave.

9th St.

Whiskey Island

Edgewater Park

Edgewater Dr.

West Blvd.

Lorain Ave.

2

90

71

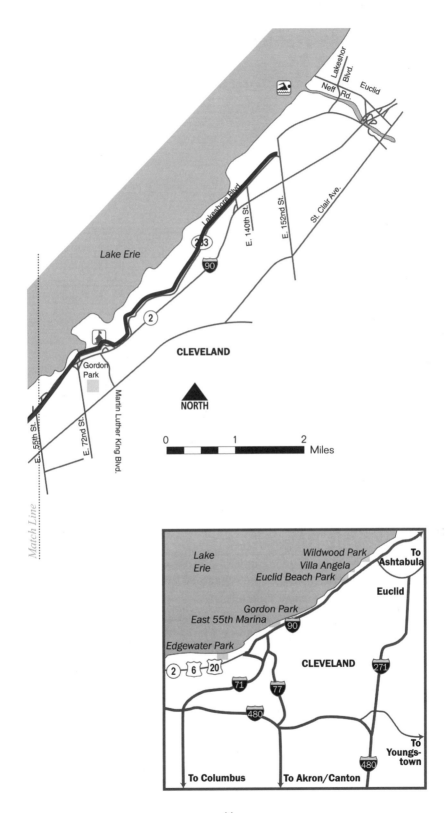

All Purpose Trails
Cleveland Metroparks

Trail Uses	🚲 🏃 🛼
Surface	Paved, some gravel
Trail Length	Over 60 miles

Trail Notes

The eastern section is hillier, with climbs that are sometimes steep and long, climbing or descending in and out of the river valley. The western section more closely follows the river and remains closer to the valley floor.

Contact

Cleveland Metroparks   216-351-6300
4101 Fulton Parkway
Cleveland, Ohio 44144

Bedford Reservation

Gorge Parkway Trail is a 5.25 mile trail from Alexander Road in Walton Hills along Overlook Lane, Gorge Parkway, and Egbert Lane to Union Street in Bedford and connects with South Chagrin Reservation via the Hawthorn Parkway. There is also a 5 mile gravel-based trail from Alexander Road in Walton Hills to Highland Road that connects with a 20 mile bike trail that serves the MetroParks of Summit County. There are entrances off Button, Dunham, Egbert, and Willis roads.

Brecksville Reservation

The Valley Parkway Trails consists of a 2.9 mile trail along Valley Parkway from Edgerton Road to Ridge Road and a 4.5 mile trail along Chippewa Creek Drive and Valley Parkway from Route 82 to Riverview Road. There are entrances off routes 82 and 21, and Riverview and Parkview roads. There are several short and fairly steep hills.

Euclid Creek Reservation

The Euclid Creek Trail is a 2.5 mile trail from the Highland Picnic Area in Euclid to Green Road in South Euclid. There are entrances off Highland and Green roads.

Garfield Park Reservation

The Garfield Park Trial is a 2.4 mile trail from Broadway Avenue to Turney Road. The Mill Creek Overlook is a 1.5 mile trail along Turney Road to Mill Creek Falls Overlook. There is an entrance off Broadway Avenue to Turney Road.

Hinckley Reservation

Hinchley Lake Trail is a 3 mile loop trail around Hinckley Lake, along West Drive, State Road, East Drive, and Bellus Road in Hinckley Township. There are entrances off Bellus and State roads.

Huntington Reservation

Porter Creek Trail is a 1 mile trail along Porter Creek Drive from Lake Road in Bay Village to Wolf Road, and from Porter Creek Drive east, past the Wolf Picnic Area connecting to the city of Bay Village's bike trail. There are entrances off Lake and Wolf roads.

South Chagrin Reservation

Hawthorn Parkway Trail is a 3.5 mile trail along Hawthorn Parkway from the Harper Ridge Picnic Area, just north of Solon Road in Solon to the Squaw Rock Picnic Area, continuing north to Chagrin River Road with a loop back along Sulphur Springs Drive to Hawthorn Parkway. There are entrances off Miles, Chagrin River, SOM Center (Route 91), Cannon, Harper, and Richmond roads.

TRAIL LEGEND	
▬▬▬▬	Trail-Biking/Multi
··············	Hiking only Trail
• • • • • • • ◖	Hiking - Multi Use
▬▬▬▬	Snowmobiling only
= = = = = = = =	Planned Trail
▨ ▨▨ ▨▨ ▨▨ ▨▨ ▨	Alternate Trail
▬▬▬▬	Road/Highway
+++++++++++	Railroad Tracks

AREA LEGEND	
▨	City, Town
▨	Parks, Preserves
▣	Waterway
◉	Marsh/Wetland
▬▬▬	Mileage Scale
★	Points of Interest
‒ ‒	County/State
♣	Forest/Woods

Cleveland Metroparks

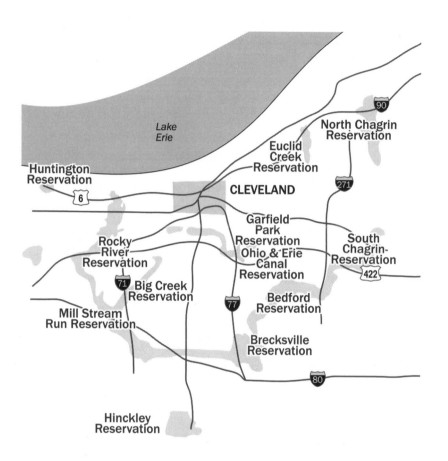

SYMBOL LEGEND	
🏊 Beach/Swimming	MF Multi-Facilities
🚲 Bicycle Repair	P Parking
🏠 Cabin	🪑 Picnic
⛺ Camping	🏛 Ranger Station
🛶 Canoe Launch	🚻 Restrooms
✚ First Aid	🏠 Shelter
🍴 Food	T Trailhead
GC Golf Course	🏛 Visitor Center
? Information	🚰 Water
🛏 Lodging	🔭 Overlook/ Observation

Big Creek Reservation

The reservation runs parallel to Pearl Road from Valley Parkway to Brookpark Road, and is located in Brooklyn, Parma, Parma Heights, Middleburg Heights, and Strongsville. It connects with the Mill Stream Run Reservation via Valley Parkway in Strongsville. The 7.5 mile trail passes through marshes, a floodplain, pine plantation, woodland, and an orchard. A highlight of the reservation is Lake Isaac. It's classified as a "glacial pothole", created thousands of years ago, and is a waterfowl refuge.

There are entrances located off Brookpark, Eastland, Snow, and Stumph roads, West 130th Street, East Bagley, Fowles, and Whitney roads and Valley Parkway.

Memphis Ave.

480

Tiedeman Rd.

Hauserman Rd.

Big Creek Pkwy.

Snow Rd.

Big Creek

Holland Rd.

Sheldon Rd.

Stumph Rd.

130th St.

Smith Rd.

Eastland Rd.

Engle Rd.

Lake Abram

Pearl Rd.

E. Bagley Rd.

NORTH

Fowles Rd.

Lake Isaac Waterfowl Sanctuary

Beyer's Pond

71

Sprague Rd.

Main St.

42

Pearl Rd.

Beech Hill Pond

Apple Ridge Pond

Valley Pkwy.

Cleveland Metroparks
Mill Stream Run Reservation

The Valley Parkway Trail is a 6.5 mile trail from Bagley Road to West 130th Street with a loop around the Bonnie Park Picnic Area.

There are entrances off Routes 42 and 82, Albion, Handle, Lee, Prospect, Eastland, Edgerton, and Bagley roads, South Rocky River Drive and West 130th Street.

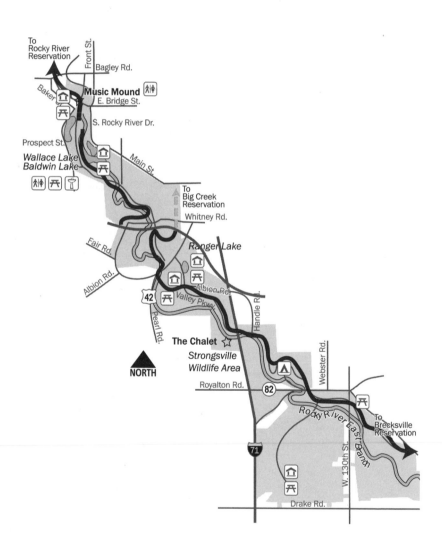

North Chagrin Reservation

Buttermilk Falls Parkway Trails is a 4 mile trail from Chardon Road in Willoughby Hills, south along Buttermilk Falls Parkway in Mayfield Village's Trails and two spurs west to SOM Center Road.

Three are entrances off SOM Center (Route 91), Chagrin River and Chardon roads.

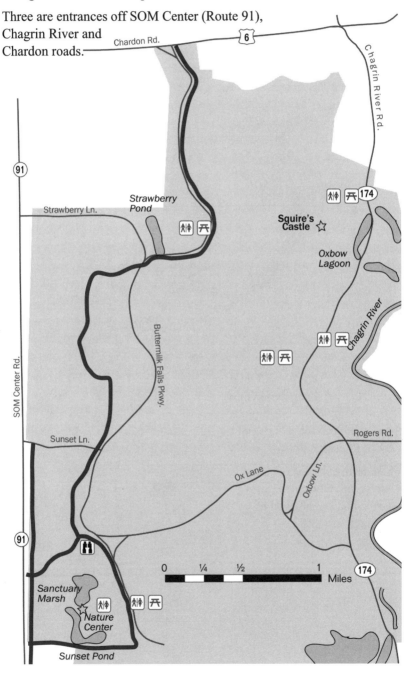

Cleveland Metroparks
Ohio & Erie Canal Reservation

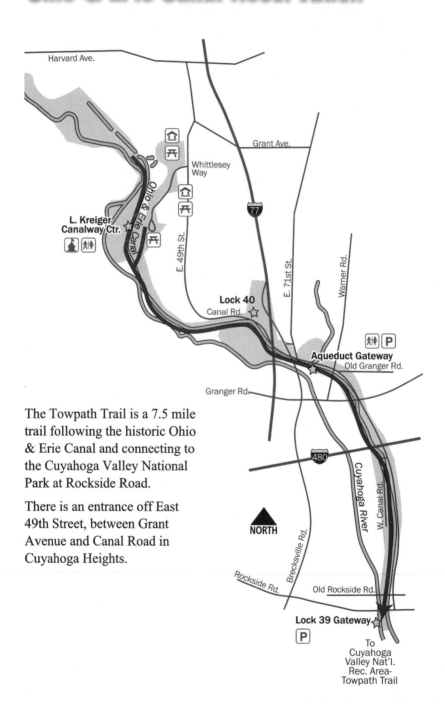

The Towpath Trail is a 7.5 mile trail following the historic Ohio & Erie Canal and connecting to the Cuyahoga Valley National Park at Rockside Road.

There is an entrance off East 49th Street, between Grant Avenue and Canal Road in Cuyahoga Heights.

Rocky River Reservation

The Valley Parkway Trail in this Reservation is a 13 mile trail from the Scenic Park Picnic Area off the Detroit Road entrance in Lakewood, south along Valley Parkway to Bagley Road in Berea, then connecting with the Mill Stream Run Reservation. Entering the reservation you descend into Rocky River Valley which is frequently at the bottom of a deep ravine. The trail travels through wooded areas and along and over several hills.

There are entrances off Detroit Road, Riverside Drive, Wooster and Mastick roads, Brookway Lane, Cedar Point, Old Lorain, Spafford, Barrett and Bagley roads, and Shepard Lane.

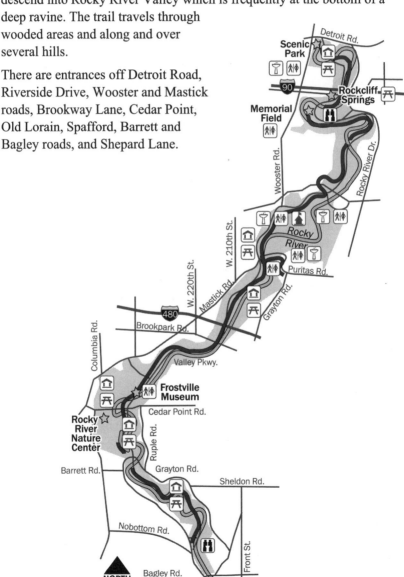

Conotton Creek Trail

Trail Uses	🚴 🏃 🛼
Area	Northern Harrison County
Trail Length	11.5
Surface	Paved

Trail Notes

The Harrison County Conotton Creek Trail is a multi-use rail-trail extending 11.5 miles through Harrison County. The eastern trailhead is near the headwaters of Conotton Creek, a stream whose waters ultimately flows through the Muskingum Valley lake to the Ohio and Mississippi rivers. Conotton Creek and the Trail meander side by side through small villages, farms, wetlands, pastures, and Ohio shale and sandstone cuts in the rolling hills of eastern Ohio. The trail connects the villages of Jewett, Scio, Conotton, and Bowerston. The trail is also intersected at two points by the Tappan-Moravian Trail Scenic Byway and adjoins the Buckeye Trail, a 1,435 mile hiking trail that loops the state.

The Conotton Valley slopes down to the west so riding the trail from west to east and back gives you a small boost on the return leg as it is mostly downhill, although the grade is very gentle. There is a parking area in Scio and restrooms are available nearby in the town park area a short distance off the trail. There is a parking lot with picnic tables, benches, and toilet at the Rumley Road crossing about 1.25 miles from the eastern end of the trail. The trailhead at Jewett has a large parking lot, picnic tables, benches, toilet and a small covered bridge nearby. There are benches frequently placed along the entire length of the trail.

Getting There

From Steubenville, take SR 22 west to where it joins with SR 151. Continue on SR 22/151 to until the they separate again. Take SR 151 northwest to the Jewett trailhead or continue west along SR 151 to Bowerston trailhead to begin your ride.

Contact

Crossroads RC&D   330-330-9317
277 Canal Avenue, SE, Ste C
New Philadelphia, OH 44663

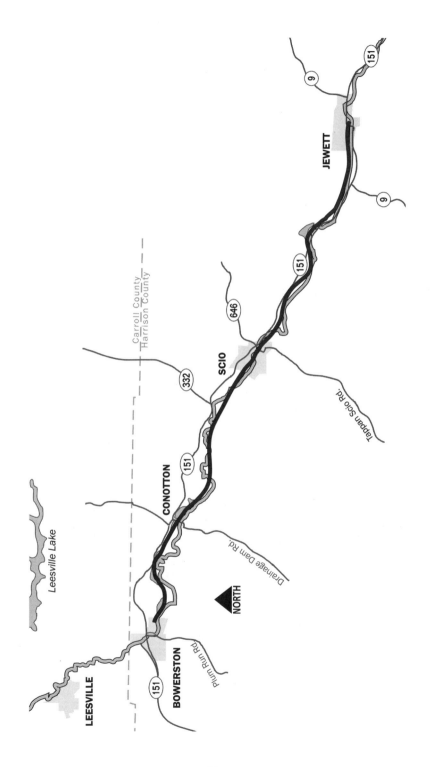

Dillon State Park

Trail Uses	🚴 🏃 ⛺
Area	Muskingum County
Trail Length	12 miles
Surface	Natural

Trail Notes

Dillon State Park has 12 miles of dedicated, interlocking loop trails that are color-coded for easy, moderate and difficult. Trailheads are located off the beach and marina parking lots, and the campground offers easy access to the trails. Green caps on posts represent easy, yellow caps represent moderate, and red caps represent difficult biking.

The wooded hills and scenic valley of the Dillon area offer a picturesque setting for your adventure. The park is situated in an area that possesses diverse features resulting from the Black Hand Sandstone. The sand eroded hundreds of years ago and accumulated in a vast delta in the sea covering the region, forming sheer cliffs and supporting a lush, hardwood forest. Facilities at the park included rental cottages, equipped campsites, a 1,360 foot swimming beach, and boating.

Getting There

From Newark take Route 16 east to SR146, then go a mile eastbound on RT 146 is Toboso Road. Take Toboso Road south to get to the beach area. Continue east on SR 146 to Ballard Road. Turn right on Ballard Road, which become Dillon Hill Road taking you to the marina area.

Contact

Dillon State Park   740-453-4377
5265 Dillon Hills Drive
Nashport, OH 43830

TRAIL LEGEND	
————	Trail-Biking/Multi
··············	Hiking only Trail
••••••••••	Hiking - Multi Use
▪▪▪▪▪▪▪▪	Snowmobiling only
==========	Planned Trail
▪ ▪ ▪ ▪ ▪ ▪	Alternate Trail
————	Road/Highway
++++++++++	Railroad Tracks

SYMBOL LEGEND

🏊	Beach/Swimming	MF	Multi-Facilities
🚲	Bicycle Repair	P	Parking
🏠	Cabin	🛏	Picnic
▲	Camping	🛡	Ranger Station
🛶	Canoe Launch	🚻	Restrooms
✚	First Aid	🏠	Shelter
🍴	Food	T	Trailhead
GC	Golf Course	🏛	Visitor Center
?	Information	🚰	Water
🛏	Lodging	🔭	Overlook/Observation

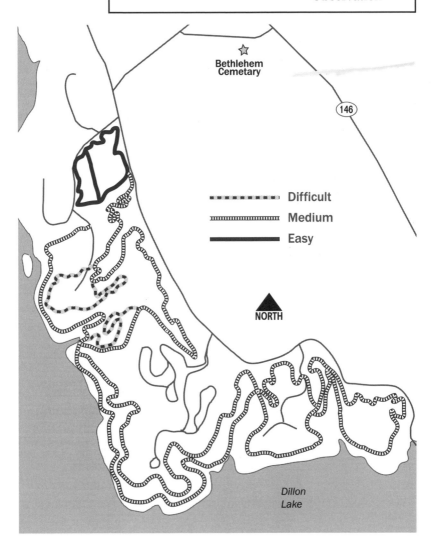

☆
Bethlehem Cemetary

146

············· Difficult
ᴨᴨᴨᴨᴨᴨᴨᴨᴨ Medium
━━━━━━ Easy

▲
NORTH

Dillon Lake

East Fork State Park

Trail Uses   🚵 🏃 🐴

Area	Bethel
Trail Length	6 miles
Surface	Natural

Trail Notes

East Fork is one of Ohio's largest state parks with 4, 870 acres. It's located some 25 miles from Cincinnati. The park's terrain includes rugged hills and open meadows. There is a 1,200 foot swimming beach, a campground, and picnic areas. Bike rentals are available at the campground. The 32 mile Steven Newman Worldwalker Perimeter Trail circling the park is only open to hikers, backpackers, and horsemen.

The mountain bike trails are identified with blue blazes and begins just west of the park entrance on SR-125. Effort level is easy to moderate. The trails are well maintained, and mostly flat, with only about a 100 foot change in elevation. They wind through a portion of the bottomland hardwood forest bordering East Forest Lake. It's generally a very tight singletrack. The surface can be very sloppy when wet.

Getting There

East Fork State Park is only about 25 miles east of Cincinnati off SR 125. From the north follow I-71 or I-75 south to the I-275 loop. Take the loop I-275 east and exit SR 125 east. The park entrance is on SR 222. Enter on Park Road. The trailhead is just beyond the park office on the left. Follow the short gravel road between two ponds to the parking area.

Contact

East Fork State Park   513-734-4323
3294 Elklick Road
Bethel, OH 45106

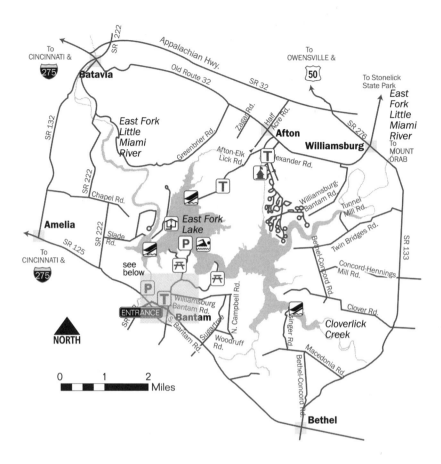

To CINCINNATI & **275**

Batavia

Appalachian Hwy.

SR 222

Old Route 32

SR 32

To OWENSVILLE & **50**

To Stonelick State Park

SR 132

East Fork Little Miami River

Greenbrier Rd.

Zagar Rd.

Afton-Elk Lick Rd.

Half Acre Rd.

Afton

lexander Rd.

T

Williamsburg

Williamsburg-Bantam Rd.

Tunnel Mill Rd.

East Fork Little Miami River To MOUNT ORAB

SR 276

SR 222

Chapel Rd.

T

Amelia

SR 222

Slade Rd.

P

East Fork Lake

Bethel-Concord Rd.

Twin Bridges Rd.

Concord-Hennings Mill Rd.

SR 133

To CINCINNATI & **275**

SR 125

see below

P

P **T**

ENTRANCE

Bantam

Williamsburg Bantam Rd.

N. Campbell Rd.

Sugartree

Clover Rd.

Clover Rd.

Cloverlick Creek

NORTH

Bantam Rd.

Woodruff Rd.

Bethel-Concord Rd.

Macedonia Rd.

0   1   2 Miles

Bethel

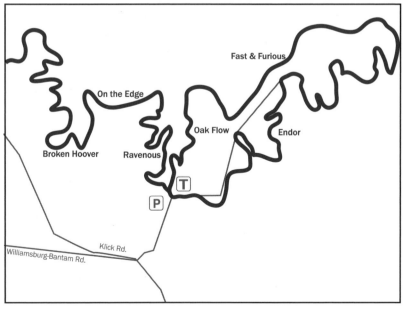

Fast & Furious

On the Edge

Oak Flow

Endor

Broken Hoover

Ravenous

T

P

Klick Rd.

Williamsburg-Bantam Rd.

Findley State Park

Trail Uses	🚲 🚶 ⛷
Area	Cleveland
Trail Length	10 miles
Surface	Natural

Trail Notes

Findley State Park is heavily wooded with stately pines and hardwoods. The scenic trails provide an opportunity to view spectacular wildflowers and observe wildlife. The fields, forest and quiet waters offer a peaceful refuge for your visit. The 10 miles of trail include a portion of the statewide Buckeye Trail.

This is a re-growth secondary forest on abandoned farmland. The forest floor supports a variety of woodland wildflowers including spring beauties, hepatica, bloodroot trillium and woodland asters. White-tailed deer, red fox, beaver and raccoon are common. This part of the state is also known as Ohio's dairyland. Facilities include a camp area with showers, flush toilets, laundry facilities, and a camp store. There is a 435 foot beach, concessions, picnic area, and marina with boat launch ramps.

Getting There

Findley State Park is located two miles south of Wellington in Lorain County. From Cleveland, take I-480 southwest to SR 58. Go south on SR 58 past Wellington to the park entrance. Follow the park road south to the camp check-in station, which can serve as a convenient trailhead.

Contact

Findley State Park 440-647-4490
25381 State Route 58
Wellington, OH 44090

AREA LEGEND	
	City, Town
	Parks, Preserves
	Waterway
	Marsh/Wetland
▪━▫━	Mileage Scale
★	Points of Interest
---	County/State
🌲	Forest/Woods

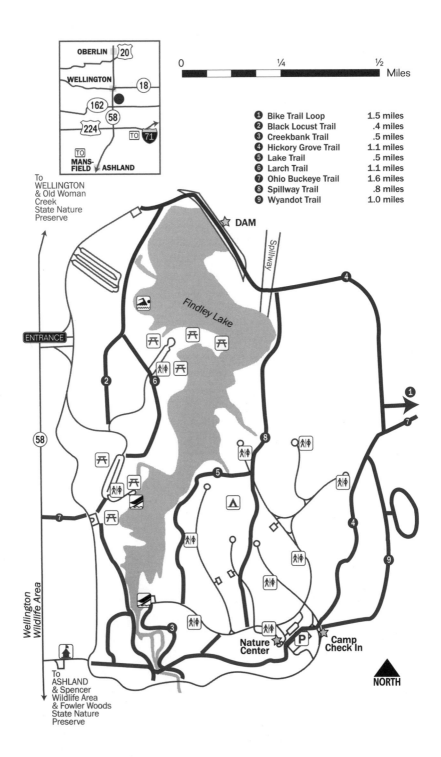

	Trail	Distance
❶	Bike Trail Loop	1.5 miles
❷	Black Locust Trail	.4 miles
❸	Creekbank Trail	.5 miles
❹	Hickory Grove Trail	1.1 miles
❺	Lake Trail	.5 miles
❻	Larch Trail	1.1 miles
❼	Ohio Buckeye Trail	1.6 miles
❽	Spillway Trail	.8 miles
❾	Wyandot Trail	1.0 miles

OBERLIN 20
WELLINGTON 18
162
58
224 TO 71
TO MANS-FIELD ASHLAND

0   ¼   ½   Miles

To WELLINGTON & Old Woman Creek State Nature Preserve

ENTRANCE

58

7

Wellington Wildlife Area

To ASHLAND & Spencer Wildlife Area & Fowler Woods State Nature Preserve

DAM

Spillway

Findley Lake

Nature Center

Camp Check In

P

NORTH

Gallipolis Bike Path
Gallia County Hike & Bike Trail

Trail Uses	🚴 🚶 ⛷ 🔦
Area	Gallipolis
Trail Length	7 miles completed, (total of 28 miles planned)
Surface	Crushed limestone (completed sections)

Trail Notes

This trail is a former CSX railway right-of-way. From its current 7 limestone surfaced miles, it will ultimately stretch 28 miles from southern Vinton County through Gallia County to Gallipolis, and extending to Kanauga. The trail features gentle grades through rolling farmland, short stretches through small towns, and over steel bridges. The completed sections are the 3.3 miles from Mill Creek Road to McCormick Road, and the 4.5 miles from Kerr Road to SR554. This area is a very mountainous and scenic part of Ohio. The southern trailhead in Gallipolis is located just north of the Ohio River, forming the border with West Virginia.

Getting There

The town of Gallipolis is 2.5 mile south of US 35 on SR 160. From Cincinnati take SR 32 east to US 35, then southeast to Gallipolis. From Columbus, take SR 23 south to US 35. There is street parking in Gallipolis, Kerr, Evergreen and Bidwell. A good starting point is the trailhead on Mill Creek Road, just north of Route 7 in Gallipolis.

Contact

McIntyre Park District   740-446-3612
18 Locust Street
Gallipolis, OH 45631

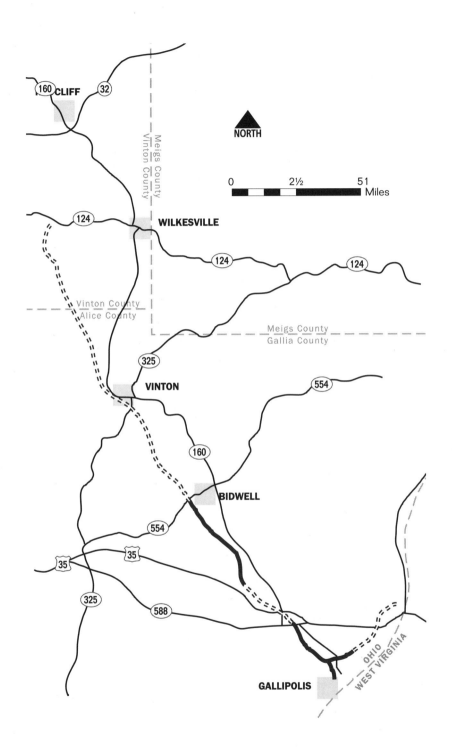

Great Ohio Lake-to-River Greenway
Western Reserve Greenway
Mill Creek Metroparks Bikeway (Canfield Rail-Trail)
Little Beaver Creek Greenway Trail

Trail Uses

Trail Notes

The Great Ohio Lake to River Greenway, when completed, will include a 100 mile River Greenway open to bicyclists, hikers, equestrians, snowmobilers, and pedestrians. It begins at West Avenue in Ashtabula where the former Pennsylvania Railroad line started and runs along that line through Ashtabula, Trumbull, Mahoning, and Columbiana counties, ending in Lisbon.

Contacts

Western Reserve Greenway   440-992-8132
134 W. 46th Street
Ashtabula, OH 44004

Ashtabula County Parks   440-576-0717
25 W. Jefferson Street
Jefferson, OH 44047

Trumbull County Metroparks   330-675-2480
347 N. Park Avenue
Warren, OH 44481

Mahoning County   330-702-3000
7574 Columbiana-Canfield Road
Canfield OH 44406

Columbiana County Park District 330-424-9078
130 W. Maple Street
Lisbon, OH 44432

Western Reserve Greenway

Area   Ashtabula to Champion

Trail Length   43 miles

Surface   Asphalt

Trail Notes

Ashtabula's section of the Western Reserve Greenway extends north from the Trumbull line about 3.4 miles to Hague Road, and from the former Penn Central rail right-of-way from Hague Road north for 5.9 miles to Callender Road. The next section of the Greenway open to the public begins at Callender Road and extends north 16.7 miles to West 5nd Street in the City of Ashtabula.

The Trumbull County Western Reserve Greenway is open from Champion East Road in Champion Township north 14.7 miles to the Ashtabula County line. Phase III of the Greenway will connect the City of Warren Trail System to Champion East Road in Champion Township.

Mill Creek MetroParks Bikeway
(Canfield Rail-Trail)

Area   Mahoning County

Trail Length   11 miles

Surface   Asphalt

Trail Notes

The Mill Creek Bikeway opened in 2000, and travels from Canfield to the Trumbull County line. The grade is gentle, increasing from the lowest point at County Line Road to the highest point at Lisbon Street in Canfield for a elevation difference of only 180 feet. It was originally constructed in the 1860's as the Niles and Lisbon Railroad, but closed to passenger traffic in the late 1930's.

The Kirk Road Trailhead provides a 50-car parking lot, restrooms, water, and a picnic pavilion. The 402 acre MetroParks Farm is located on Route 46 across from the Canfield Fairgrounds. This is a working farm, with a farm animal display barn, a hands-on AgVenture exhibit barn, and a Children's Vegetable Garden.

Getting There

Canfield can be accessed via I-70, US Routes 224 or 62.

Great Ohio Lake to River Greenway (continued)

Little Beaver Creek Greenway Trail

Area   Columbiana County

Trail Length   11 miles

Surface   Asphalt

Trail Notes

This 10 foot wide trail begins in Lisbon, and travels along the rail bed of the former Erie Lackawanna Railroad to Leetonia. It is nestled in hardwood forest that runs along scenic Little Beaver Creek. In the summer, the tree canopy transforms the trail into a virtual tunnel that keeps the trail cool and comfortable during the heat of the day. Lisbon is the site of the terminal moraine (front edge) of the Wisconsin Glacier, the most recent glacier to make it to this part of the country.

While this bikeway is a rail-trail, it does have some elevation variation. Near Lisbon, the trail takes a ½ mile detour over the road, which is clearly marked. Toward Leetonia there are a few small wooden decked bridges that are a little rough to ride. About half way through the ride there is an old covered bridge near the trail on Eagleton Road. Several picnic tables and benches are provided along the trail, and most of the trail is fenced from the surrounding woods. Traffic is generally light at the several road crossings you will experience.

Getting There

State Routes 30, 164, 154, 11, 517 and 164 all junction in Lisbon. There is a parking area with a porta-potty at the trailhead.

Leetonia is located just south of the Columbiana/Mahoning County borders and can be accessed via State Routes 344or 164.

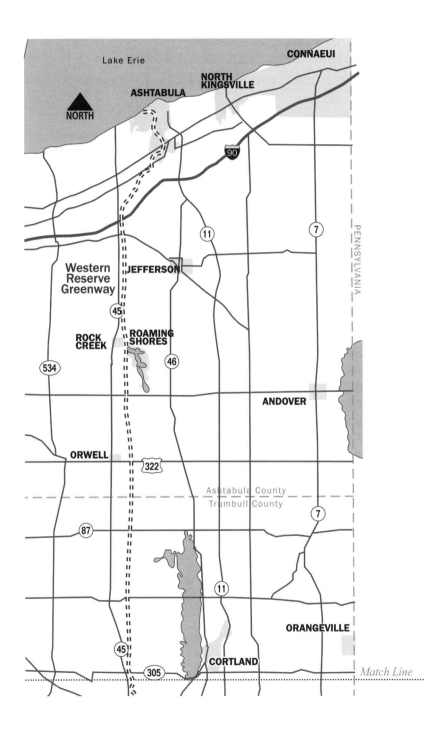

Lake Erie

CONNAEUI

NORTH KINGSVILLE

ASHTABULA

NORTH

90

11

7

PENNSYLVANIA

Western
Reserve
Greenway

JEFFERSON

45

ROCK
CREEK

ROAMING
SHORES

46

534

ANDOVER

ORWELL

322

Ashtabula County
Trumbull County

7

87

11

ORANGEVILLE

45

CORTLAND

305

Match Line

Great Ohio Lake to River Greenway (continued)

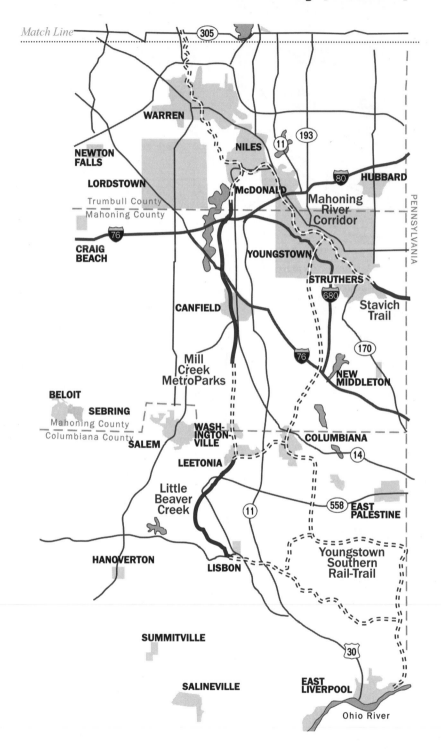

Match Line

WARREN

NEWTON FALLS

NILES

LORDSTOWN

McDONALD

HUBBARD

Mahoning River Corridor

Trumbull County
Mahoning County

CRAIG BEACH

YOUNGSTOWN

STRUTHERS

Stavich Trail

CANFIELD

Mill Creek MetroParks

NEW MIDDLETON

BELOIT

SEBRING

Mahoning County
Columbiana County

SALEM

WASH-INGTON-VILLE

COLUMBIANA

LEETONIA

Little Beaver Creek

EAST PALESTINE

HANOVERTON

LISBON

Youngstown Southern Rail-Trail

SUMMITVILLE

SALINEVILLE

EAST LIVERPOOL

Ohio River

PENNSYLVANIA

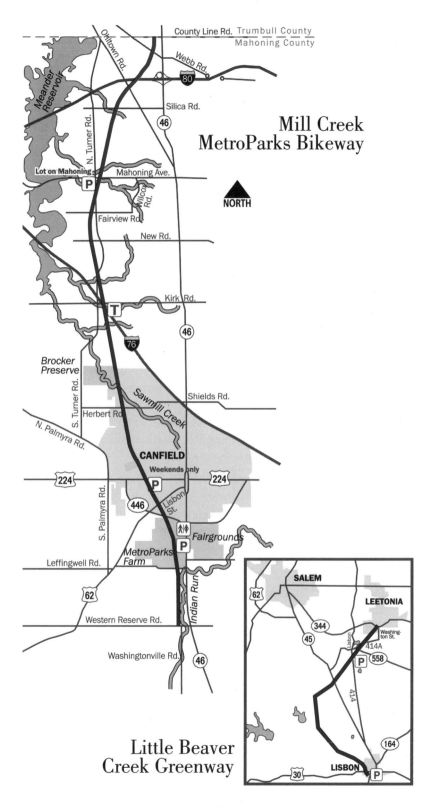

Mill Creek MetroParks Bikeway

NORTH

County Line Rd. — Trumbull County / Mahoning County
Webb Rd.
80
Okltown Rd.
Silica Rd.
46
Meander Reservoir
N. Turner Rd.
Lot on Mahoning P
Mahoning Ave.
Wilcox Rd.
Fairview Rd.
New Rd.
Kirk Rd.
T
76
46
Brocker Preserve
S. Turner Rd.
Herbert Rd.
Shields Rd.
Sawmill Creek
N. Palmyra Rd.
CANFIELD
Weekends only
224
224
P
S. Palmyra Rd.
446
Lisbon St.
P Fairgrounds
MetroParks Farm
Leffingwell Rd.
62
Western Reserve Rd.
Indian Run
Washingtonville Rd.
46

SALEM
62
344
45
LEETONIA
Washington St.
414A
P 558
414
Leffingwell
164
30 LISBON P

Little Beaver Creek Greenway

65

Great Seal State Park

Trail Uses	🚴 🏃 🎿 🎧
Area	Chillicothe
Trail Length	22 miles
Surface	Natural

Trail Notes

The park's challenging trails will take you to scenic vistas of distant ridgetops and the Scioto Valley below. These are the hills depicted on the Great Seal of Ohio, from which the park got its name. The terrain varies from steep to gently rolling.

The Sugarloaf Mountain Trail (yellow) is 2.1 miles long, and climbs through dense maple forests to the crest of Sugarloaf. This loop rises almost 500 feet in less than a quarter mile. Shawnee Ridge Trail (blue) is 7.8 miles long, and comprises Bald Hill, Sand Hills and parts of Rocky Knob. There are several steep sections in this forested trail. Mt. Ives Trail (orange) is 6.4 miles long, and winds along Mt. Ives, providing several scenic vistas. Effort level for this trail would be rated as difficult. Spring Run is 3.4 miles long and is designated for hiking. The 1.1 mile long Picnic Loop and the 1 mile long Grouse Rock trails are limited to hiking only.

The Great Seal State Park lies upon the Appalachian escarpment, a line of hills stretching across Ohio's mid section, which outline the edge of the Appalachian plateau in the state. North and west of the line are glaciated plains while south and east rugged hills extend to the foothills of the mountain.

Getting There

Great Seal State Park is located just north of the town of Chillicothe. Take State Route 159 north to Delano Road, turn right and go to the Marietta Road intersection, then turn right to the park entrance.

From Cleveland, take I-71 South to I-270 West to US 23 South (Circleville Exit). Proceed south on 23, through Circleville 17 miles to the Delano Exit. Follow signs to the park entrance, located 3 miles east off US 23.

From Columbus, take US 23 South through Circleville 17 miles to the Delano Exit. Follow signs to the park, which is located 3 miles east off of US 23.

From Cincinnati, take US 50 East to Chillicothe, then US 23 North to State Route 159. Turn right on Delano Road and follow signs to the Park, which is located 2 miles north of Chillicothe.

From Toledo, take US 23 to Columbus to I-270. Take I-270 West to the US 23 Exit. Go south through Circleville 17 miles to Delano Road Exit. Follow the signs to the park.

Contact

Great Seal State Park   740-663-2125
144 Lake Road
Chillicothe Oh, 45601

Harbin Park Mountain Bike Trail

Trail Uses	🚵
Area	Fairfield
Trail Length	5.5 miles
Surface	Natural

Trail Notes

Located in Fairfield, not far from Cincinnati. The trails consist of 2 loops – an orange marked trail and a green marked trail. The trails are almost entirely wooded single track. They are generally very smooth and hard packed dirt with some serious technical sections riddled with rocks, logs and roots. The trail is tight and twisty and has some short steep climbs. The descents can be fast. The trails are well maintained, in cooperation between the Cincinnati Off Road Alliance and the park.

The start of the 3 mile orange trail is at the park entrance. Follow the orange markings until they end at the frog pond. To find the start of the 2.5 mile long green trail go to the highest ground and look for the blue water tank. As you approach the tank look for the green trail markings. The sledding hill adds another distance to the ride. Both the orange trail and the green trail connect and end at the frog pond.

Getting There

To get there from Cincinnati take I-275 to the Mt. Healthy exit and proceed north on SR-127 for about 5 miles and turn left at Hunter Road. Hunter Road dead-ends into the park entrance.

Contact

Harbin Park
513-867-5348

SYMBOL LEGEND

🏊	Beach/Swimming	MF	Multi-Facilities
🚲	Bicycle Repair	P	Parking
🏠	Cabin	🎋	Picnic
⛺	Camping	🧍	Ranger Station
🛶	Canoe Launch	🚻	Restrooms
+	First Aid	🏠	Shelter
🍴	Food	T	Trailhead
GC	Golf Course	🏛	Visitor Center
?	Information	🚰	Water
🛏	Lodging	🔭	Overlook/ Observation

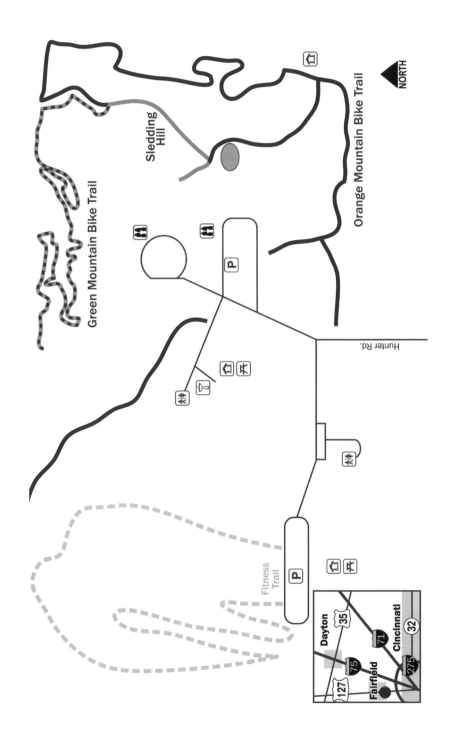

Green Mountain Bike Trail

Orange Mountain Bike Trail

Sledding Hill

Fitness Trail

Hunter Rd.

NORTH

Dayton

Cincinnati

Fairfield

35

71

32

75

275

127

Hockhocking Adena Bikeway

Trail Uses	🚴 🥾 🛼 🏃
Area	Athens
Trail Length	19 miles
Surface	Asphalt

Trail Notes

The Hockhocking Adena Bikeway is located on the old Columbus and Hocking Valley Railroad bed between Athens and Nelsonville. "Hockhocking" which means "bottleneck" or "twisted", was the native Adena Indian name for the Hocking River. This paved rail-trail nestles between the Hocking River, and the large cliffs and scenic rock outcroppings as it winds through the forest. The trail passes along the Hocking Canal, through Beaumont, and the campus of Ohio University. Repeated flooding in the late 1800's severely damaged portions of the canal, but remnants of the canal basin are still visible from the bikeway, particularly from Armitage north to Chauncey.

Getting There

The Athens trailhead is located off of East State Street at the city park, just east of US Hwy 33. You can also start your ride in Nelsonville on the campus of Hocking College at a reconstructed pioneer village.

Contact

Hockhocking Adena Bikeway   800-878-9767
667 E. State Street
Athens, OH 45701

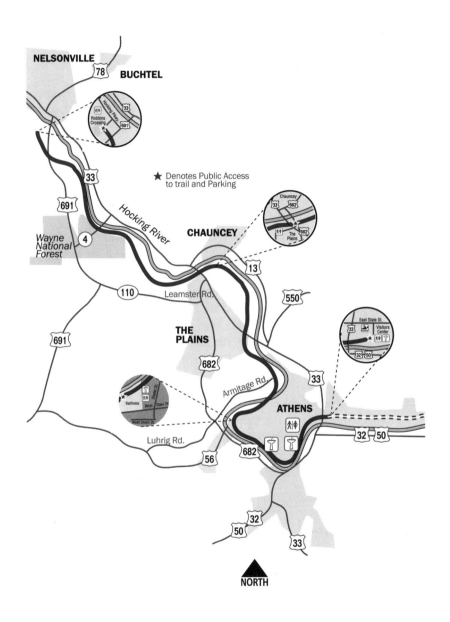

★ Denotes Public Access
to trail and Parking

NORTH

Holmes County Trail

Trail Uses	🚲 🏃 ⛷ 🛼 🎧
Area	Millersburg
Trail Length	12 miles
Surface	Asphalt, natural

Trail Notes

This unique dual-purpose trail is shared with Amish buggies. The section between Millersburg and Fredericksburg was completed in 2005. It is partially asphalt paved 10 foot, and partially chip and seal. Three phases remain, Brinkhaven to Glenmont, 7.5 miles, currently open only for hiking. Glenmont to Killbuck, about 7 miles long, is closed for all uses. Killbuck to Millersburg is open for mountain biking and hiking. When completed the trail will total approximately 29 miles and be 10-14 feet wide.

The trail near downtown Millersburg bends to avoid a large parking area just before it moves under Route 39. The new Millersburg Depot, named Hipp Station, is just past the highway bridge. At Route 83, there is a lighted tunnel under the roadway. You'll find a restroom and food stop nearby by taking the asphalt spur to the right before entering the tunnel. The combination surface flip-flops on occasion, moving the horse & buggy side from left to the right side and visa versa. The trail passes through woods, open fields and wetland on its way to Fredericksburg.

Getting There

Millersburg is located at the junction of Routes 39 and 83. If you're starting out from Millersburg, there is parking at the local WalMart. The trail connects to the parking lot to allow Amish horse & buggies access to the trail.

Contact

Holmes County Rails-to-Trails   330-279-2643
PO Box 95
Millersburg, OH 44654

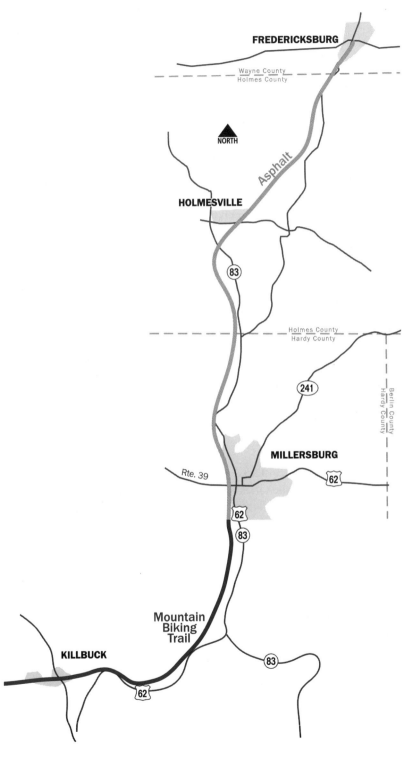

FREDERICKSBURG

Wayne County
Holmes County

NORTH

Asphalt

HOLMESVILLE

83

Holmes County
Hardy County

241

Berlin County
Hardy County

MILLERSBURG

Rte. 39

62

62

83

Mountain
Biking
Trail

KILLBUCK

83

62

Hueston Woods State Park

Trail Uses	🚲 🏃 ⛷ 🎧
Area	North of Cincinnati & west of Dayton
Trail Length	14 miles
Surface	Natural

Trail Notes

The nearly 3,000 acre Hueston Woods State Park is located in Butler & Preble counties, near the Indiana State Line. The park surrounds Acton Lake. In addition to mountain biking, activities include hiking, horseback riding, cross-country skiing, canoeing, golf, and fossil hunting. Facilities include campsites, cabins, and a resort lodge. The American Discovery Trail also passes through the park. Call for trail and rental information.

This is a singletrack trail with some challenging uphills and downhills, in addition to several creek crossings, stumps, and even ramps. The woodland settings offer a great mix of difficulty and terrain, from dense woods, to open meadows and views of Action Lake. The trails are well marked, and generally well maintained. There are several opportunities to access the park roads during your ride. The effort level is mostly moderate, and the trails are well marked with green, blue, or red. Bike rentals are available at the bike shop. The horse trails are separate, but they do pass the bike trails once.

Getting There

From Dayton, take I-75 south to Hwy 725. Follow 725 west through Gratis and Camden, then look for the Hueston Woods signs. Bear right on the Main Loop Road. Julie's Bike Shop is on the right beside the trailhead, where you can stop for advice on trail options.

From Oxford, take College, which becomes Brown Road to the park, then left on the Main Loop Road until you see the bike shop.

Contact

Hueston Woods State Park	513-523-6347
6301 Park Office Road	
College Corner, Ohio 45003	
Julie's Bike Rentals	513-523-1316

Power Line

Huron River Greenway

Trail Uses   🚲 🥾 🎿

Area	Huron
Trail Length	6 miles (13 miles when complete)
Surface	Limestone screenings

Trail Notes

This multi-use trail is constructed on what was once the Milan Canal. The canal closed in 1869 and the towpath became the right-a-way for the Wheeling and Lake Erie Railway, which itself became deactivated. The trail is signed, and runs along the east bank of the Huron River in Erie County. From Huron, it follows River Road between US Route 6 and the trailhead parking area south of the SR-2 overpass to Mason Road. The setting is woodlands and scenic wetlands. Currently there is about a one mile unfinished gap in the trail on either side of I-80/90. When completed the pathway will connect the shore of Lake Erie in Huron to the planned North Coast Inland Trail at Norwalk. There are observation decks along the trail overlooking marshlands and forested areas.

The trail is open daily from 8 am to dark. Currently there is no drinking water on the trail, and only seasonal restroom facilities.

Getting There

From Huron, take River Road south about two miles. Cross the railroad tracks, and you'll see a water tower on the right. The trailhead to the Huron River Greenway is at the base of the tower. There also is parking area on Main Street in Milan.

Contact

Erie MetroParks   419-625-7783
3910 Perkins Avenue
Huron, OH 44839

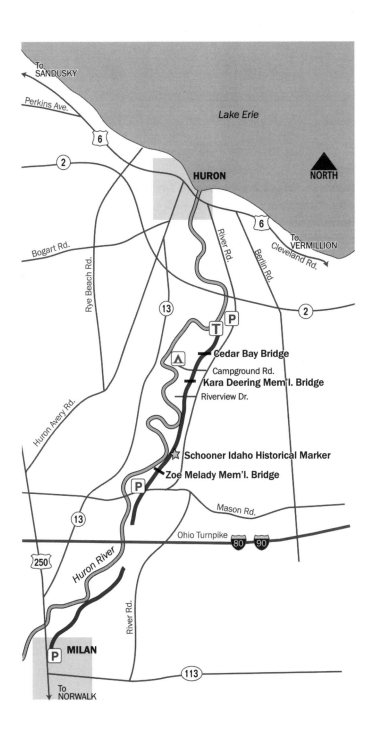

Jefferson Lake State Park

Trail Uses	🚵 🚶 ⚲
Area	Steubenville
Trail Length	22 miles
Surface	Natural, groomed

Trail Notes

The 962 acre State Park is located in Jefferson County, 10 miles northwest of Steubenville and within an hour's drive southeast of Canton. The 22 miles of scenic, multiple-use trails meandering through the park are rugged and sometimes challenging. Horses seem to be more common than bikers. The wider equestrian trails are sometimes muddy in the lower areas, but overall are in pretty good shape. There are steep climbs and long, fast downhills. The Downhill Trail is probably the more technical of the trails you will experience.

The sandstone hills of Jefferson County are part of the Appalachian Highlands, which cover the southeastern part of Ohio. The forest is composed of second growth oak and hickory with beeches, maples, tulip trees, elms, walnuts and ashes. It is not unusual to see wild turkey and ruffed grouse along your ride. Facilities include camping, boating, swimming, and picnicking. The public beach offers a bathhouse, showers and toilets.

Getting There

From Steubenville, take Alternate 22 west to SR 43. Proceed northwest to State Park Road. Go north on State Park Road for about a mile to the park entrance.

Contact

Jefferson Lake State Park   740-765-4459
501 Township Road 261 A
Richmond, Ohio 43944

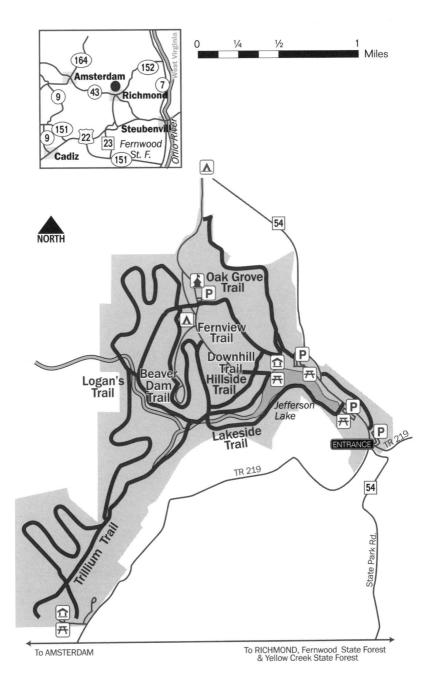

John Bryan State Park

Trail Uses	🚴 🏃 ⛰️
Area	Between Springfield & Xenia
Trail Length	8.5 miles
Surface	Crushed stone, natural-groomed

Trail Notes

There are 8.5 miles of mountain biking trails at the park open to mountain biking. The trails were built and are maintained by the Miami Valley Mountain Bike Association in partnership with the Park. The line trail opened in April 2002. Two other trails, Abracadabra and Great Scott, opened in April 2003. There were 7.5 miles of trail through 2005, with another mile being added in 2006. There is also a Skills Park with technical trail features to test balance and agility. All trails are contiguous and multi-purpose. They are marked with signs, have some log jumps and the creek crossings may we wet or dry depending on the weather.

Power Line is 1.5 miles with twisty turns and long runs, some creek crossings and a small ramp. Follow the Arboretum trail starting at the kiosk and take the first left to Power Line.

Abracadabra is 2.5 miles of flat and fun riding. It has one medium-sized ramp (with a bypass around it), a boardwalk, and small creek crossings. Follow Arboretum and take the first right to Abracadabra. Abracadabra starts directly across from the Power Line exit.

Great Scott is the longest trail at 3.5 miles and has some small climbs, creek crossings, several boardwalks and the biggest ramp (with a bypass around it). Great Scott is the second right off of Arboretum. It starts directly across from Abracadabra and finishes behind the big gravel parking lot near the kiosk.

Recommended Route is clockwise: Start at the kiosk, take Arboretum & go left on Power Line. Complete Power Line & go across Arboretum to Great Scott. Follow Upper Great Scott to Lower Great Scott, cross the big creek bridge to the Great Scott loop & return by the road, cross the creek & return to Lower Great Scott & the parking lot. Follow the arrows at intersections for the recommended route.

The Miami Valley Mountain Bike Association asks that you help track trail usage by signing the Trail User Log at the Arboretum trailhead kiosk, where you can find trail maps and other park information.

John Bryan is probably the most scenic state park in western Ohio, especially with its remarkable limestone gorge cut by the Little Miami River. Activities include rock climbing and rappelling, boating and fishing. There is a day-use lodge, picnic areas and camping, some with electrical hookups.

Getting There
Follow US 68 to just north of Yellow Springs. Go east on 343 for 3 miles & turn right on Meredith (or SR 370) to John Bryan State Park.

Contact
John Bryan State Park   937-767-1274
3790 State Route 370
Yellow Springs, OH 45387

John Bryan State Park Trail

Courtesy of Karen Wells-Hamilton and the Miami Valley Mountain Bike Association

John Bryan State Park (continued)

John Bryan State Park – Final Race

Courtesy of Karen Well-Hamilton and the Miami Valley Mountain Bike Association

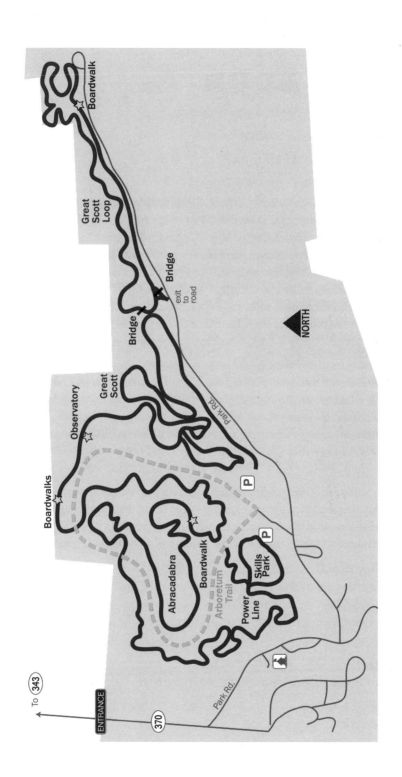

Kokosing Gap Trail

Trail Uses	🚲 🏃 ⛸ 🚶
Area	Mount Vernon, Danville
Trail Length	13.5 miles
Surface	Asphalt

Trail Notes

This is a recently surfaced 13.5 mile, 10 foot wide trail running between Mt. Vernon and Danville. Most of the trail is tree-lined with the Kokosing River weaving its way alongside. There are several river crossings on wooden-decked steel bridges, providing some scenic views. A couple of these bridges have built-in observation decks where you can stop and enjoy the view without blocking the trail. Posts mark the trail distance every half mile, and street name signs have been erected at most of the road crossings. There are restrooms and water stations in Mt. Vernon at Phillip's Park, Gambler, and at the stone arched bridge in Howard.

In Gambler the trail passes along the edge of a college campus, and past a display of an old steam engine, coal car, flatbed and caboose. In Howard, you will pass through a stone-arched tunnel at Route 36. Heading to Danville the scenery changes to farmland, with some hills, woods and pastures. In Danville, the Mohican Valley starts only a few blocks from where the Kokosing ends. There are signs to help direct you.

There is also a .4 mile segment beginning on Mt. Vernon Avenue, just opposite the trail along the Kokosing River Dike, that heads west and will eventually work its way over to Route 13 near downtown Mt. Vernon. It will connect to the Ohio-to-Erie Trail network from the southeast.

Getting There

The Mt. Vernon trailhead is at Phillips Park off Liberty Street. There is a large parking lot along Mt. Vernon Avenue. To get to the extension heading into downtown Mt. Vernon, cross the bridge at Mt. Vernon Avenue.

Contact

Knox County Visitor's Bureau   740-392-6102

Kokosing Gap Trail
PO Box 129
Gambier, Ohio 43022

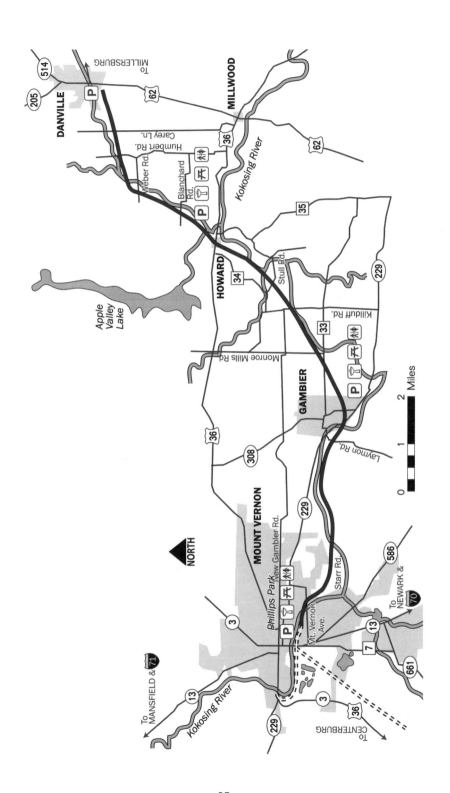

Lake Hope State Park

Trail Uses   🚵 🚶 🎧

Area   Athens, Vinton County

Trail Length   23 miles

Surface   Natural, groomed

Trail Notes

Lake Hope State Park lies within the 26,824 acre Zaleski State Forest in the valley of Big Sandy Run. The setting is rugged, forested and traversed by steep gorges and narrow ridges. Attractions include abandoned mines, ancient mounds and beautiful scenery. Lake Hope's 23 mile singletrack bike trail was chosen as Ohio's top mountain bike trail by readers of "Mountain Bike Magazine". This wooded area has plenty of riding options. The trails are maintained in large part by the Athens Bicycle Club.

Activities and facilities include a rustic dining lodge, cottages, camping, boating, fishing, a swimming beach, and the Hope School House Interpretive Center. The second-growth forest is dominated by oak and hickory trees, while the woodland floor harbors an assemblage of shrubs and wildflowers such as the yellow lady's slipper, blue-eyed mary and bloodroot. You may also observe deer, wild turkeys and beavers along your ride. The Hope Furnace was built in the mid 19th century to process the iron ore extracted from the region's sandstone bedrock. Today, the Hope Furnace chimney and some of the foundation are all that remain of the structure.

Getting There

From Athens, take SR 56 west to SR 278 just past the Vinton/Hocking County line. Take SR 278 south about 7 miles to the park entrance on your right.

From Chillicothe, take US 50 east to SR 677. Proceed north on SR 677 to the small community of Zaleski. Continue north on US 278 to the park entrance.

Contact

Lake Hope State Park   740-596-5253
27331 State Route 278
McArthur, OH 45651

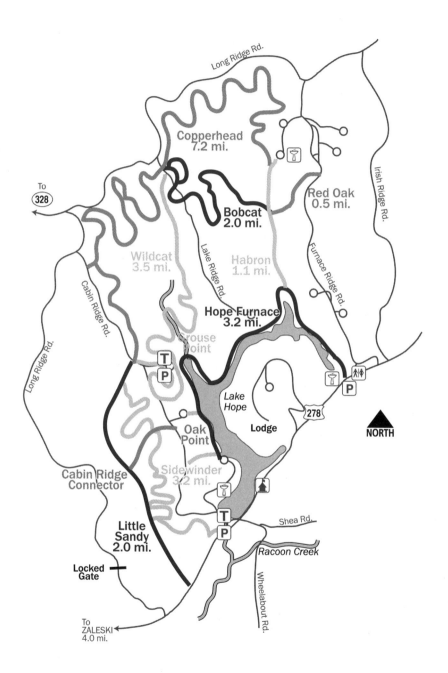

Long Ridge Rd.

Copperhead
7.2 mi.

Irish Ridge Rd.

To
328

Red Oak
0.5 mi.

Bobcat
2.0 mi.

Wildcat
3.5 mi.

Lake Ridge Rd.

Habron
1.1 mi.

Furnace Ridge Rd.

Cabin Ridge Rd.

Hope Furnace
3.2 mi.

Long Ridge Rd.

Grouse
Point

T
P

Lake
Hope

278

Oak
Point

Lodge

NORTH

Cabin Ridge
Connector

Sidewinder
3.2 mi.

T
P

Shea Rd.

Little
Sandy
2.0 mi.

Racoon Creek

Locked
Gate

Wheelabout Rd.

To
ZALESKI
4.0 mi.

Lebanon Countryside Trail

Trail Uses   🚲 🏃 🛼 ⛷️

Area	Lebanon
Trail Length	8.2 miles
Surface	Asphalt

Trail Notes

The trail starts in downtown Lebanon near the train station, runs east toward the Armory and then turns south into Harmon Park where it passes over Turtle Creek on a bridge. The trail then continues east to the SR48 bypass, turning south toward the Warren County government complex and from there through the city past the Countryside YMCA, and Kings View/Fujitec Road. Continue south, crossing Tuttle Creek on a bicycle bridge, and then back onto the old "Middletown Junction" rail-bed until it crosses the Little Miami River to connect with the Little Miami Scenic Trail.

While the Lebanon Countryside Trail is scenic it is also quite hilly. It is generally downhill from downtown south to the Little Miami Scenic Trail, but there are several very steep hills especially from Deerfield Road South and after you pass the YMCA. A part of the trail takes you on Deerfield Road. The trail is marked on the shoulder of the road on each side.

Getting There

Lebanon Trailhead – Take SR 48 & 42 South through downtown Lebanon past the Golden Lamb Hotel and the Warren County Historical Society Museum to South Street and turn left. The trailhead is just past the depot.

Contact

Lebanon Parks & Recreation   513-932-3060
50 South Broadway
Lebanon, Ohio 45036

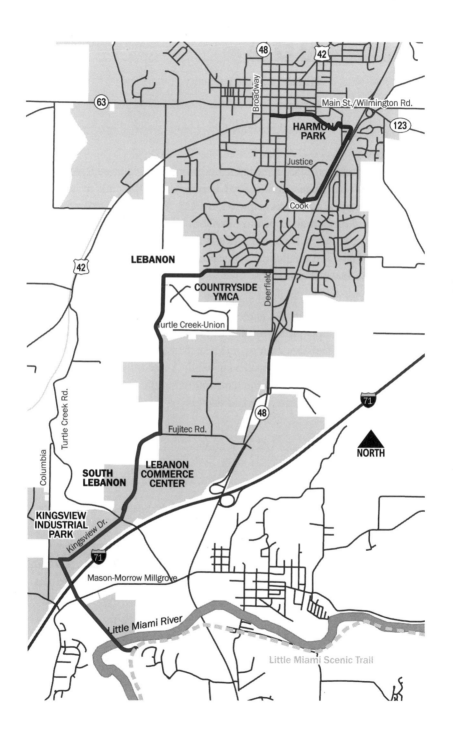

Mary Jane Thurston State Park

Trail Uses   🚴 🏃 🐴

Area	Napoleon, Henry County
Trail Length	6 miles
Surface	Natural, groomed

Trail Notes

Mary Jane Thurston State Park is located along the Maumee River straddling Wood, Lucas, and Henry Counties in the flatlands of northwest Ohio. The original park was acquired in 1928. The North Turkeyfoot Area, located upriver and open to mountain biking, was acquired as additional parkland in 1968. Facilities at the park include camping, a marina, boating, and picnicking. The area is steeped in Native American and Revolutionary War history.

The 6 miles of trail are flat and easy with no technical challenges. Each trail in the network bears the name of a mammal, such as the Red Fox Trail, Whitetail Loop and so forth. Parking is available at the Pheasant Loop Trailhead. The elevation gain is less than 80 feet. The trail is open to backpackers and horseback riders as well. A one mile portion of the Buckeye Trail passes through the park following the side cut canal, and continues on to the Village of Grand Rapids.

Getting There

From the Toledo area, take US 24 southwest to the North Turkeyfoot Area.

Contact

Mary Jane Thurston State Park   419-832-7662
1-466 SR 65
McClure, Ohio 43534

TRAIL LEGEND	
————————	Trail-Biking/Multi
··············	Hiking only Trail
•••••••••••◄	Hiking - Multi Use
▪▪▪▪▪▪▪▪▪	Snowmobiling only
==========	Planned Trail
▬ ▬ ▬ ▬ ▬ ▬	Alternate Trail
————————	Road/Highway
+++++++++++	Railroad Tracks

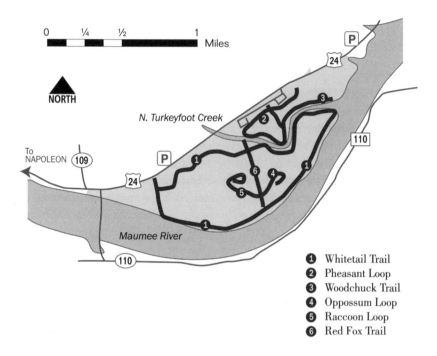

0   ¼   ½   1
Miles

NORTH

N. Turkeyfoot Creek

P
24

To
NAPOLEON 109

P

24

110

1

1

6   4

5

1

110

Maumee River

1. Whitetail Trail
2. Pheasant Loop
3. Woodchuck Trail
4. Oppossum Loop
5. Raccoon Loop
6. Red Fox Trail

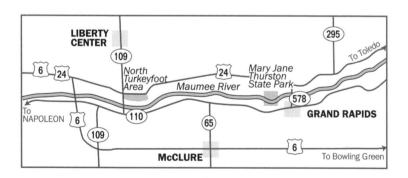

LIBERTY
CENTER

109

295

To Toledo

6   24

North
Turkeyfoot
Area

24

Mary Jane
Thurston
State Park

Maumee River

578

To
NAPOLEON   6

110

65

GRAND RAPIDS

109

McCLURE

6

To Bowling Green

Montgomery County's Trails
Great Miami River Recreation Trail
Wolf Creek Recreation Trail
Stillwater River Recreation Trail
Mad River, Creekside Recreation, & Kettering Recreation Trails

There are over 60 miles of scenic, multi-use trails in Montgomery County. They were built and are maintained by the Miami Conservancy District, Five Rivers Metro Parks and several local communities. This trail system is part of a multi-county, interconnected trail network linking to the Greene County trail system and eventually north to Piqua in Miami County, south to Hamilton in Butler County and west into Preble County.

Trail Rules & Regulations
Bicyclists must yield to all other users.

Keep right except to pass

Announce that you are passing so as not to startle others

Move off the paved trail when stopped so that other may continue unobstructed

Pets must be ona leash. Remove all pet droppings from the trail and dispose of them far from the trial's edge.

All Trails close at dark and open at dawn

Motorized vehicles and horse are prohibited on trails

Dispose of trash in provided receptacles

Contact
Miami Conservancy District   937-223-1271
38 E. Monument Ave.
Dayton, OH 45402

Five River Metro Parks   937-275-7275
1375 E. Siebenthaler Ave.
Dayton, OH 45414

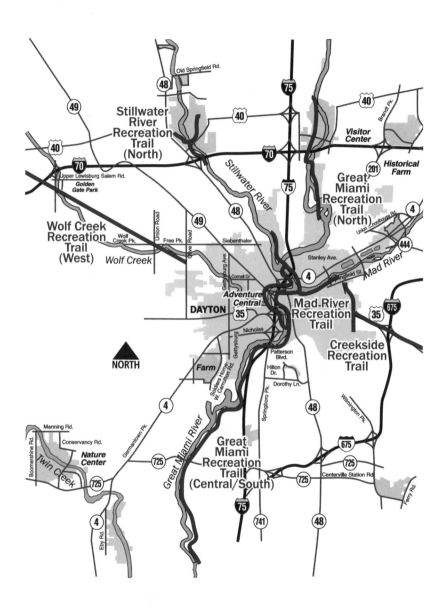

93

Montgomery County's Trails
Great Miami River Recreation Trail

Trail Uses	
Area	Dayton
Trail Length	30 miles
Surface	Asphalt

Trail Notes

The Great Miami River Recreation Trail winds its way near museums, picnic facilities, acres of nature parkland and gently rolling terrain. The Southern Segment follows the Great Miami River and passes through the communities of Oakwood, Kettering, West Carrollton and Miamisburg. The Central System passes through downtown Dayton, past numerous monuments, RiverScape, and historic parks. The Northern Segment wanders through the heavily wooded Taylorsville Metro Park and along the Great Miami River, past Taylorsville Dam and Tadmor historic site.

North Segment

94

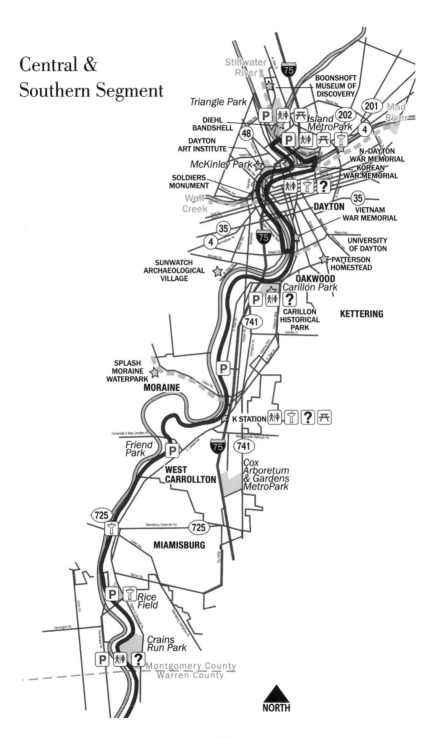

Central & Southern Segment

Stillwater River

BOONSHOFT MUSEUM OF DISCOVERY

Triangle Park

DIEHL BANDSHELL

DAYTON ART INSTITUTE

Island MetroPark

McKinley Park

SOLDIERS MONUMENT

N. DAYTON WAR MEMORIAL
KOREAN WAR MEMORIAL

Wolf Creek

DAYTON

VIETNAM WAR MEMORIAL

UNIVERSITY OF DAYTON

SUNWATCH ARCHAEOLOGICAL VILLAGE

PATTERSON HOMESTEAD

OAKWOOD
Carillon Park

CARILLON HISTORICAL PARK

KETTERING

SPLASH MORAINE WATERPARK

MORAINE

K STATION

Friend Park

WEST CARROLLTON

Cox Arboretum & Gardens MetroPark

MIAMISBURG

Rice Field

Crains Run Park

Montgomery County
Warren County

NORTH

Wolf Creek Recreation Trail

Trail Uses   🚲 🏃 ⛷ 🛼

Area	Dayton
Trail Length	15.5 miles
Surface	Asphalt

Trail Notes

The Wolf Creek Recreation Trail was built on the CSX railroad bed running from Trotwood through Brookville to Verona. The asphalt surface is 12 feet wide, and the grade is gentle. The trail passes over two bridges, a large limestone culvert, and through Sycamore State Park. Plans include extending the trail to Greenville, and southeast to the Great Miami River Recreation Trail.

The Trotwood trailhead is at the Trotwood Station, which has parking, restroom and water facilities, although the trail actually continues southeast of the station for another half mile or so. Starting from Trotwood Station, you will first cross Union Road and Main Street, both of which have signal-changing buttons. There also is parking in Brookville at Golden Gate Park (the entrance is off Upper Lewisburg Salem Road one block south of the I-70 exit), and in Verona at the Village Park (located off Preble County Line Road, about four blocks north of the trail). Restrooms and drinking water are available at all the staging areas except during freezing weather.

The ride from Trotwood follows a slightly uphill grade for most of the way to Brookville. The scenery is open country with field and countryside views for most of the way to Verona. As you approach Verona, the trail becomes tree-lined. It ends at the Preble County Line Road.

Getting There

To get to the Trotwood trailhead, take I-70 West from Dayton to SR 49 (Salem Road), and then south on SR 49 to Union Road. Turn south (right) on Union Road to the Station in Trotwood at Union Road and Main Street.

Contact

Five Rivers MetroParks   513-275-7275
1375 E. Siebenthaler
Dayton, OH 45414

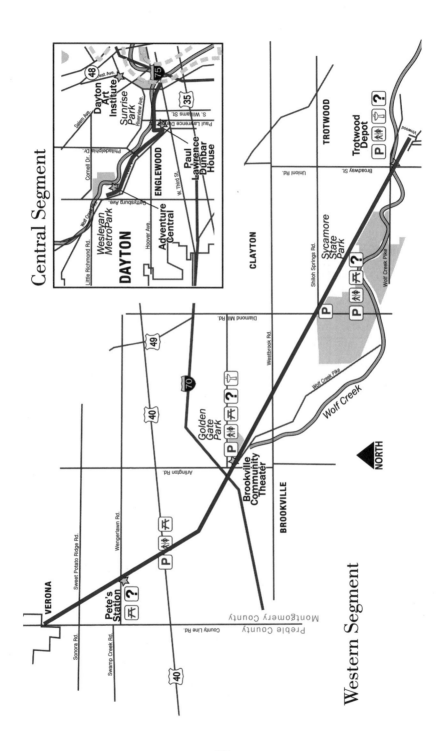

Central Segment

DAYTON

Wesleyan MetroPark

Dayton Art Institute

Sunrise Park

ENGLEWOOD

Paul Lawrence Dunbar House

Adventure Central

Western Segment

VERONA

Pete's Station

BROOKVILLE

Brookville Community Theater

Golden Gate Park

CLAYTON

Sycamore State Park

TROTWOOD

Trotwood Depot

Wolf Creek

NORTH

Preble County
Montgomery County

Montgomery County's Trails
Stillwater River Recreation Trail

Trail Uses   🚲 🏃 ⛷ 🛼

Area	Dayton
Trail Length	8 miles
Surface	Asphalt

Trail Notes

The Stillwater River Recreation Trail provides you a setting in a serene and diverse terrain. Lining the banks of the Stillwater River are some of the region's largest stands of sycamore, maple and ash trees. They are lush in the spring and summer, and ablaze with color in the fall.

The Central Segment starts in Island Metro Park and runs past the Diehl Bandshell on its way across the bridge through Triangle Park and along Deweese Parkway, home to the Boonshoft Museum of Discovery. Further on, the trail passes through Wegerzyn Gardens Metro Park and ends at Sinclair Park, just west of Shoup Mill Road.

The North Segment connects Grossnickle Park to Englewood Metro Park. It passes through the relief spillway of the Conservancy District's earthen dam, along the base of the dam, and winds it way through Englewood Metro Park, ending at US Route 40. There is also a spur northward to Englewood Metro Park's West Park.

SYMBOL LEGEND

🏊	Beach/Swimming	MF	Multi-Facilities
🚲	Bicycle Repair	P	Parking
🏠	Cabin	🎪	Picnic
△	Camping	🧍	Ranger Station
🛶	Canoe Launch	🚻	Restrooms
+	First Aid	🏠	Shelter
🍴	Food	T	Trailhead
GC	Golf Course	🏢	Visitor Center
?	Information	🚰	Water
🏨	Lodging	🔭	Overlook/ Observation

Northern Segment

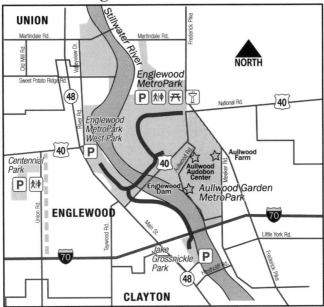

Central Segment

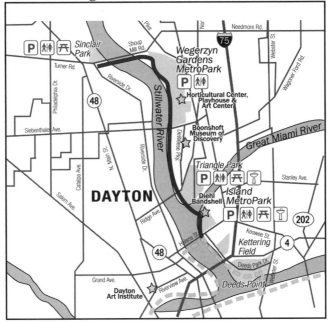

Montgomery County's Trails

Creekside Recreation Trail
Kettering Recreation Trail
Mad River Trail

Trail Uses   🚲 🚶 ⛷ 🛼

Area	Dayton	
Trail Lengths	Creekside Rec. Trail	4.6 miles
	Kettering Rec. Trail	1.9 miles
	Mad River Trail	2.8 miles
Surface	Asphalt	

Trail Notes

Creekside Recreation Trail

This trail starts at the Montgomery County/Greene County line and heads west along US 35, then turns north to Eastwood Metro Park. The trail follows an old railroad line most of the way. The ride includes a number of trail bridges and rest stations. At the county line, you can also head east on the Greene County trail system to Beavercreek, Xenia, and beyond.

Kettering Recreation Trail

You can head south from the Creekside Recreation Trail, continue under US 35, and venture along this trail as it winds its way to Spaulding Road in Kettering.

Mad River Recreation Trail

The entire length of this trail relatively flat, offering an easy workout and a great way to get from Eastwood Metropark to downtown Dayton and RiverScape. The Mad River Recreation Trail begins at Eastwood Metro Park and runs along the Mad River before joining the Great Miami River Recreation Trail at Webster Street near downtown Dayton.

Contact

River Rivers Metroparks 937-275-7275
1375 E. Siebenthaler Ave.
Dayton, OH 45414

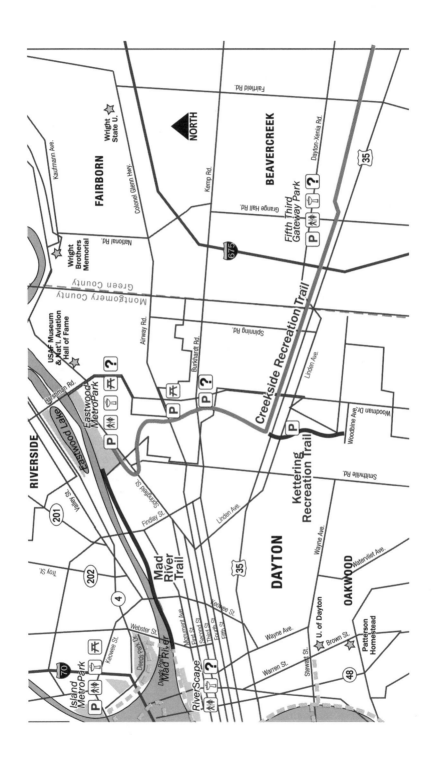

North Coast Inland Trail

Trail Uses	🚲 🏃 ⛺ 🚶
Area	Elyria, Toledo
Trail Length and Surface	Total – 65 miles of which some 20 are surfaced Lorain County section – 14.5 miles, asphalt surface Sandusky County section – 6.5 miles, asphalt surface

Trail Notes

The North Coast Inland Trail encompasses 65 miles from Elyria to Toledo. This is a planned 12 foot wide, asphalt trail, to be built over the abandoned Toledo, Norwalk and Cleveland Railroad. In 1992, seven park districts agreed to develop a system of connecting trails making up the North Coast Inland Trail.

Lorain County section: This portion runs from Elyria to Kipton, passing through Oberlin along the way. The trail passes through a variety of countryside, including farmland, fields, and forest areas. There are 24 intersections along the route, providing places to enter or exit the trail. Parking is permitted in designated areas only. Roadside parking is prohibited. Connections can be made to the Black River Reservation by following the bike route signage posted by the City of Elyria. The Black River Reservation's Bridgeway Trail is another 3.5 miles of 12 foot wide asphalt path leading to the City of Lorain.

In the Great Kipton Train Wreck of April 23, 1891, two trains collided head-on fifty feet east of the Kipton depot, killing eight people. The collision was blamed on the station engineer's watch being slow by four minutes, which caused him to miscalculate when to move one of the trails on to a side track. This incident resulted in new regulations for railroad time tracking and the creation of a quality timekeeper – the Ball Railroad Watch.

Sandusky County section: This portion of the North Coast Inland Trail runs from just east of Fremont to Clyde. You can access the trail from the East Side Biggs-Kettner Park in Fremont, or at the gazebo in downtown Clyde.

Contact

Lorain County Metro Parks 12881 Diagonal Road LaGrange, Ohio 44050	440-458-5121
Sandusky County Park District 1970 Countryside Place Fremont, OH 43420	419-334-4495

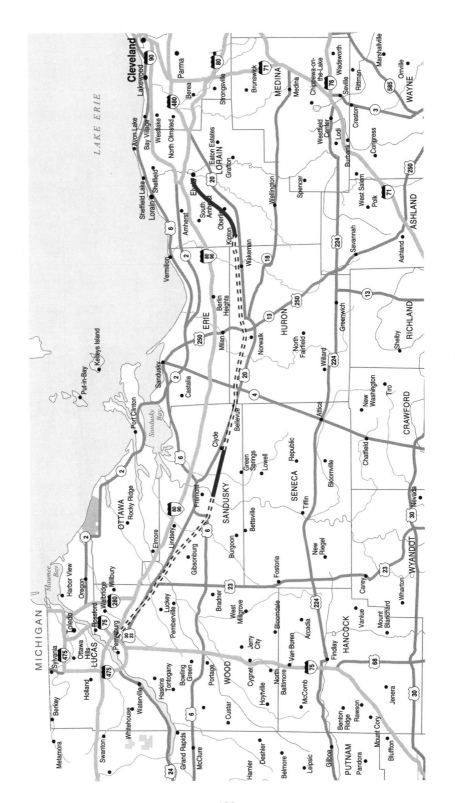

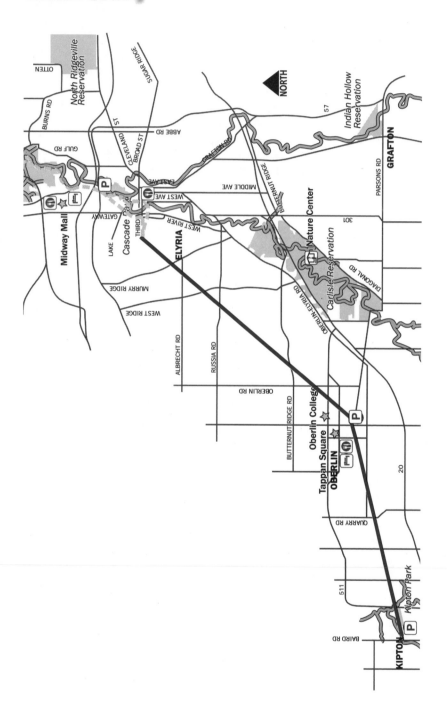

Lorain
County
Area

LAKE ERIE

Sheffield Lake • • Avon Lake
Lorain • Sheffield •
Bridgeway Trail

6

Vermillion River Greenway

Amherst • Elyria
80 90 South • Amherst
80

Oberlin 20
Kipton •
North Coast Inland Trail

Eaton Estates •

• Grafton

Wellington

Buckeye Trail

LORAIN

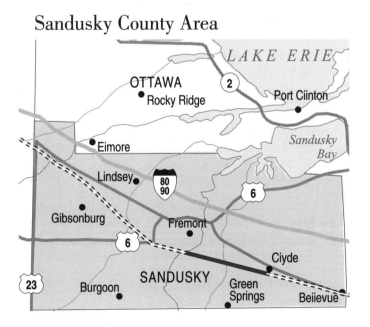

Sandusky County Area

LAKE ERIE

OTTAWA 2
• Rocky Ridge
Port Ciinton •

Eimore • Sandusky Bay

Lindsey • 80 90
6

Gibsonburg •
Fremont •
Ciyde •

23
Burgoon •
SANDUSKY
6
Green Springs
Beiievue

Oak Openings Preserve Metropark

Trail Uses   🚴 🏃 🛼 🏃 🔦

Area   Toledo

Trail Length 5.3 miles

Surface   Paved

Trail Notes

The combination of the Oak Openings Bicycle Trail with the Wabash-Cannonball Trail and Connector totals 5.3 miles of all-purpose trail. Oak Openings supports more than 1,000 different plants and the largest collection of endangered species in the state. The oak savanna dominates the landscape, which is carved with yellow quartz sand. It is the largest conservation area in the region, with living sand dunes and an interpretive center.

In addition to the all-purpose trails, there are 14.5 miles of horse trail, 16 miles of hiking trail, and some 11 miles of walking/hiking trails. The preserve is open year-round.

Getting There

Go west from Toledo on SR 2. Approximately 10 miles west of I-475 on SR 2 turn south on Girdham Road, which leads through the heart of the park.

From the north, take Hwy 23 South to Airport Highway West exit. Take Airport Highway past the Airport 295 South, and turn left off Airport Highway (look for Charlie's Restaurant on the corner). Travel past the restaurant and veer to the right at Wilkins Road. Look for park signs for your destination.

From the south take US 24 to 295 North. Stay on 295 past Route 64. Evergreen Lake is the 1st turn entrance, but go past Evergreen Lake to Oak Opening Parkway at the next entrance. Turn on Oak Openings Parkway and continue to your destination.

From the east take the turnpike from 280 South Gate 5, and go west to Gate 3A which is Route 2 (Airport Highway) exit. Turn right to Route 295, and veer to the right at Wilkins Road. Look for your desired parking area.

Contact

Oak Openings Preserve Metropark   419-826-6463
4139 GirdhamRoad
Wanton, OH 43558

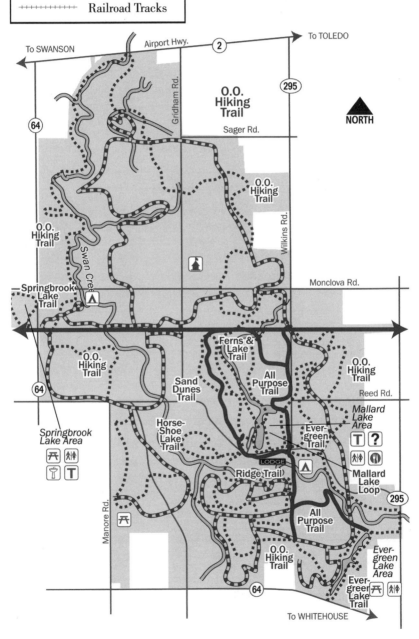

TRAIL LEGEND

————	Trail-Biking/Multi
··············	Hiking only Trail
••••••••••	Hiking - Multi Use
▪▪▪▪▪▪▪▪	Snowmobiling only
=========	Planned Trail
▬ ▬ ▬ ▬	Alternate Trail
————	Road/Highway
+++++++++	Railroad Tracks

▪▪▪▪▪▪▪▪ **Horse Trail**

To SWANSON
Airport Hwy.
(2) To TOLEDO
(295)

NORTH

(64)

O.O. Hiking Trail

Gridham Rd.

Sager Rd.

O.O. Hiking Trail

Wilkins Rd.

O.O. Hiking Trail

Swan Creek

Springbrook Lake Trail

Monclova Rd.

Ferns & Lake Trail

O.O. Hiking Trail

O.O. Hiking Trail

Sand Dunes Trail

All Purpose Trail

O.O. Hiking Trail

Reed Rd.

(64)

Mallard Lake Area

Horse-Shoe Lake Trail

Evergreen Trail

Springbrook Lake Area

LODGE

Ridge Trail

Mallard Lake Loop

(295)

Manore Rd.

All Purpose Trail

O.O. Hiking Trail

Evergreen Lake Area

Evergreen Lake Trail

(64)

To WHITEHOUSE

Ohio to Erie Trail

The Ohio to Erie Trail, when complete, will span the state of Ohio from Cincinnati to Cleveland on routes formerly owned by railroads and canals. This trial system will eventually connect four of Ohio's metropolitan cities, a dozen large towns and numerous small villages. Of the 453 miles making up this system, over 260 miles have been completed, with the remaining miles under development or in some planning stage.

The trail system passes through rural area, farmlands, nature preserves and parks. At metropolitan perimeters, meadows and woods give way to urban centers. The trails are open to bicyclists, hikers, equestrians, cross-country skiers, and other groups.

For this publication, we are presenting 5 surfaced segments of the trail system:

> Ohio & Erie Towpath Trail
>
> Licking County Recreations
> (Incorporates the T. J. Evans & Panhandle Trails)
>
> Heritage Rail-Trail
>
> Prairie Grass Trail
>
> Little Miami Scenic Trail

Contact

Ohio & Erie Canal Association   440-546-5927
1556 Boston Mills Road
Peninsula, OH 44264

① Ohio to Erie Towpath
② Thomas J. Evans Trail
③ Heritage Trail
④ Prairie Grass Trail
⑤ Little Miami Scenic Trail

Ohio to Erie Trail
Ohio & Erie Towpath

Trail Uses   🚲 🏃 🛼 🛶

Area   Cleveland to Dover

Trail Length   65 miles

Surface   Asphalt, limestone screenings, under development

Trail Notes

The Towpath Trail follows the historic route of the Ohio & Erie Canal. The canal, built between 1825 and 1832, provided a transportation route from Cleveland, on Lake Erie, to Portsmouth, on the Ohio River. The stone monuments located along the towpath denote the historic distance on the canal from the port of Cleveland on Lake Erie, and are located at approximately one mile increments. Your ride will take you by numerous wayside exhibits that provide information about canal features and sites of historic interest. You can still see remnants of the canal locks and related structures. From the trail you can also take in the beauty of forest, fields, and wetlands flanking the path as it winds its way through the Cuyahoga River Valley. Evidence of beavers, such as bark chewed off the base of tree trunks, can be seen in many places along the trail.

Contact

Ohio & Erie Canal Association   216-320-1825
PO Box 609479
Cleveland, OH 44109

SYMBOL LEGEND	
🏖 Beach/Swimming	MF Multi-Facilities
🔧 Bicycle Repair	P Parking
🏚 Cabin	🎪 Picnic
Ⓐ Camping	🏛 Ranger Station
🛶 Canoe Launch	🚻 Restrooms
✚ First Aid	🏠 Shelter
🍴 Food	T Trailhead
GC Golf Course	🏛 Visitor Center
❓ Information	💧 Water
🛏 Lodging	🔭 Overlook/ Observation

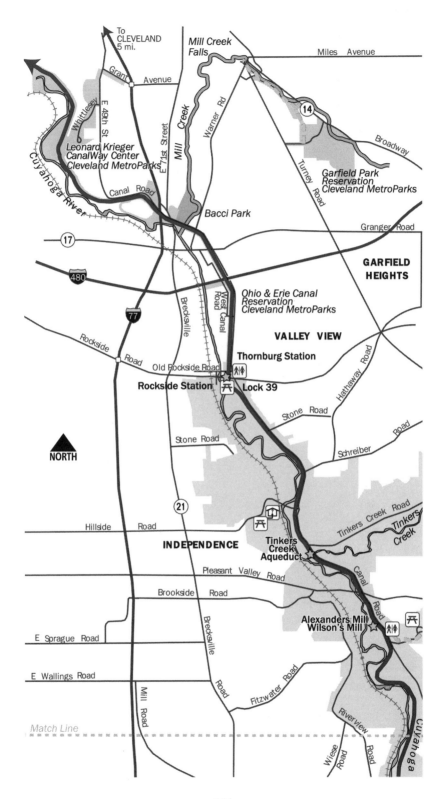

To CLEVELAND 5 mi.

Mill Creek Falls

Miles Avenue

Grant Avenue

Whittlesey

E 49th St

Mill Creek

Warner Rd

14

Broadway

Cuyahoga River

Leonard Krieger CanalWay Center Cleveland MetroParks

Canal Road

E 71st Street

Turney Road

Garfield Park Reservation Cleveland MetroParks

Bacci Park

Granger Road

17

GARFIELD HEIGHTS

I-480

Brecksville Road

West Canal Road

Ohio & Erie Canal Reservation Cleveland MetroParks

VALLEY VIEW

I-77

Rockside Road

Old Rockside Road

Thornburg Station

Rockside Station

Lock 39

Hathaway Road

Stone Road

Road

NORTH

Stone Road

Schreiber

21

Tinkers Creek Road

Tinkers Creek

Hillside Road

INDEPENDENCE

Tinkers Creek Aqueduct

Pleasant Valley Road

Brookside Road

Brecksville

Canal Road

Alexanders Mill Wilson's Mill

E Sprague Road

E Wallings Road

Mill Road

Road

Fitzwater Road

Riverview Road

Cuyahoga

Wiese Road

Match Line

111

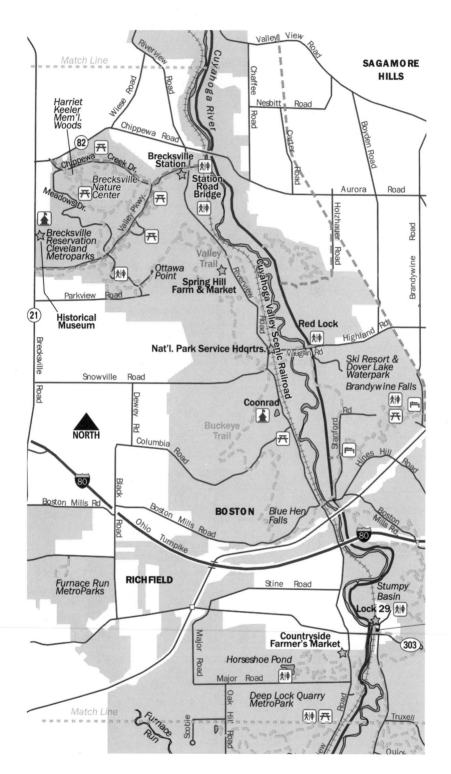

SAGAMORE HILLS

Harriet Keeler Mem'l. Woods

Chippewa Road

Valley View Road

Chaffee Road

Nesbitt Road

Carter Road

Bowden Road

Riverview Road

Wiese Road

Cuyahoga River

82

Chippewa Creek Dr.

Brecksville Station

Station Road Bridge

Aurora Road

Holzhauer Road

Brandywine Road

Brecksville Nature Center

Meadows Dr.

Valley Pkwy.

Brecksville Reservation Cleveland Metroparks

Ottawa Point

Valley Trail

Spring Hill Farm & Market

Riverview Road

Cuyahoga Valley Scenic Railroad

Parkview Road

21

Historical Museum

Red Lock

Highland Rd.

Nat'l. Park Service Hdqrtrs.

Vaughn Rd.

Brecksville Road

Snowville Road

Dewey Rd

Coonrad

Buckeye Trail

Rd.

Ski Resort & Dover Lake Waterpark

Brandywine Falls

▲ NORTH

Columbia Road

Stanford Road

Hines Hill Road

80

Black Road

Boston Mills Rd

Boston Mills Road

BOSTON

Blue Hen Falls

80

Boston Mills Rd.

Ohio Turnpike

Furnace Run MetroParks

RICHFIELD

Stine Road

Stumpy Basin

Lock 29

303

Major Road

Countryside Farmer's Market

Horseshoe Pond

Major Road

Oak Hill Road

Deep Lock Quarry MetroPark

Truxell

Match Line

Match Line

Furnace Run

Scioto

Quick

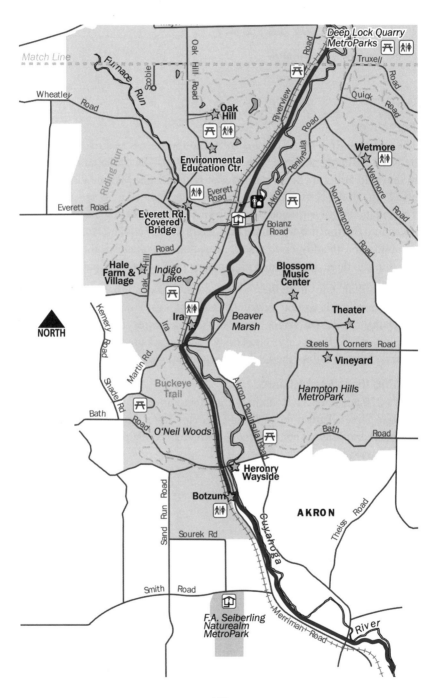

Match Line

Deep Lock Quarry MetroParks

Truxell Road

Furnace Run

Oak Hill Road

Scobie

Riverview Road

Wheatley Road

Quick Road

Oak Hill

Akron Peninsula Road

Wetmore

Wetmore Road

Environmental Education Ctr.

Northampton Road

Everett Road

Everett Road

Everett Rd. Covered Bridge

Bolanz Road

NORTH

Road

Hale Farm & Village

Indigo Lake

Blossom Music Center

Kemery Road

Oak Hill

Ira

Beaver Marsh

Theater

Steels Corners Road

Martin Rd.

Vineyard

Buckeye Trail

Akron Peninsula Road

Hampton Hills MetroPark

Shade Rd.

Bath

O'Neil Woods

Bath Road

Road

Heronry Wayside

Sand Run Road

Botzum

AKRON

Guyahoga

Theiss Road

Sourek Rd

Smith Road

F.A. Seiberling Naturealm MetroPark

Merriman Road

River

Ohio to Erie Trail
Heritage Rail-Trail

Trail Uses   🚲 🏃 ⛸ 🏃

Area   Hilliard

Trail Length   8.5 miles

Surface   Asphalt

Trail Notes

The Heritage Rail-Trail is an 8.5 mile multipurpose trail stretching between Hilliard and Plain City in central Ohio. The trailhead is located in the "Old Hilliard" historic district of Hilliard. The historic district is also home to the Northwest Historical Village located in Weaver Park. The village portrays pioneer living from 1850 to 1900. Two and half miles into the trail from Hilliard on Cosgray Road is "The Homestead", a public park. In addition to water, restroom, and picnic facilities, you can tour the three quarter mile picturesque path around the park.

To get to Plain City from the end of the trail, make a left onto Cemetery Pike and follow it around a curve to the right, pass a cemetery and cross the Darby Creek. Turn right onto Plain City-Georgesville Road and follow this into Plain City. The Darby Township Cemetery is on your right and you'll follow the Darby Creek into town.

Getting there from Hilliard

Exit I-270 at Cemetery Road in Hilliard, and go west on Cemetery Road to Main Street. Turn right on Main Street to Center Street. You can park at Center and Main. The trailhead is at the rear of the parking area next to the Makoy Center.

Contact

Heritage Rail-Trail Coalition   614-876-9554
4675 Cosgray Road
Hilliard, Ohio 43026

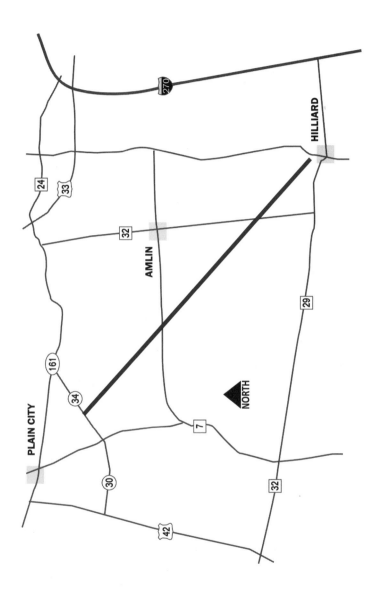

Licking County Recreation Trails
Thomas J. Evans Trail
Panhandle Trail

Trail Uses   🚲 🏃 🛼 🏃 🕳️

Area	Newark, Johnstown, Hanover	
Trail Length	Thomas J. Evans	14.3 miles
	Panhandle	8.9 miles
	Other Trails	15.5 miles
Surface	Asphalt	

Trail Notes

Thomas J. Evans Trail

The trail traverses Licking County from east to west, running from Newark to Johnstown through woods, pastures and farmlands, with occasional glimpses of Raccoon Creek that runs alongside. Most of the bikeway is lined with tunnel-like foliage, providing protection from the sun and a buffer from the wind. The trail is primarily flat, making only a gradual descent for several miles. The scenery becomes progressively more hilly as you approach Newark. The ride also takes you by historic Granville, with its restored homes, old-fashioned inns, and Denison University.

Getting There

The trailhead of the rail-trail is at Main Street and James Road, just west of Newark.

Panhandle Trail

This 10 mile, asphalt, 10-11 foot wide trail parallels SR 16 going east from Newark through Marne to Hanover. The Panhandle Trail follows the Licking River valley downstream for the first stretch before rising overland toward the northeast. It runs past the multi-story Longabarger Basket Office Building, to Felumlee Road east of Hanover near the Muskingum-Licking County line. The Panhandle is tree and brush-lined with a chain link fence and railway track running along the south side of the trail. The western section is more urban with heavier traffic, while the eastern section is more remote and secluded, passing through woods as it passes by the small community of Hanover. See the Blackhand Gorge Trail to connect to that trail from the Panhandle Trail.

Getting There

The eastern trailhead is at North Morris, just off East Main. The western trailhead is in east Newark, at Marne & Felumlee Road, just north of Marne Road.

Contact

Licking County Parks
740-587-2535
PO box 590
Granville, OH 43023

From/To	Mileage
Johnstown to Newark	14.3
Reddington Rd. (Newark) to Cherry Valley Lodge	0.5
Cherry Valley Lodge to YMCA	3.3
Newark Campus to J. Gilbert Reese Bridge	0.7
Country Club Dr. parking lot to Goosepond	2.1
Branch Path to Baker Blvd. 0.6	
Campus Path to Lefevre Hall	0.1
Campus Path to Ponds	0.2
Everett Ave. to Manning St.	1.4
Panhandle Trail - Newark to Marine	5.2
Panhandle Trail - Marine to Felumlee Rd.	4.7
Blackhand Gorge	4.2
Heath Trails	1.4
Total	**38.7**

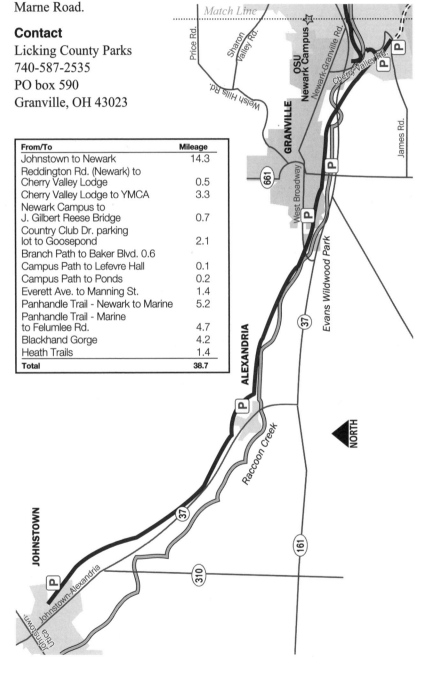

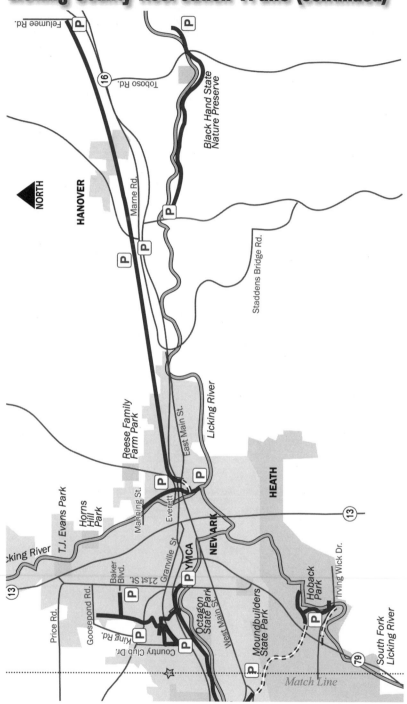

Prairie Grass Trail
Xenia to South Charleston

Trail Uses	🚲 🏃 🛼 ⛷ ⛷
Area	Xenia, South Charleston
Trail Length	18 miles
Surface	Asphalt

Trail Notes

This 10 foot wide multi-purpose trail segment of the Ohio to Erie Trail system runs from Xenia, through Cedarville, to South Charleston on a gradual uphill grade. The trail generally parallels Route 42. It gently winds through area farm fields and crosses a magnificent wooded gorge with limestone cliffs and mature hardwood forest. Xenia once served as the hub from which railroads converged from five different directions.

Getting There

The trail begins at Xenia Station, located off Detroit Street, west of US 68 and south of Federal Road.

Contact

Greene County Park District   937-376-7440
651 Dayton-Xenia Road
Xenia, OH 45385

XENIA

CEDARVILLE

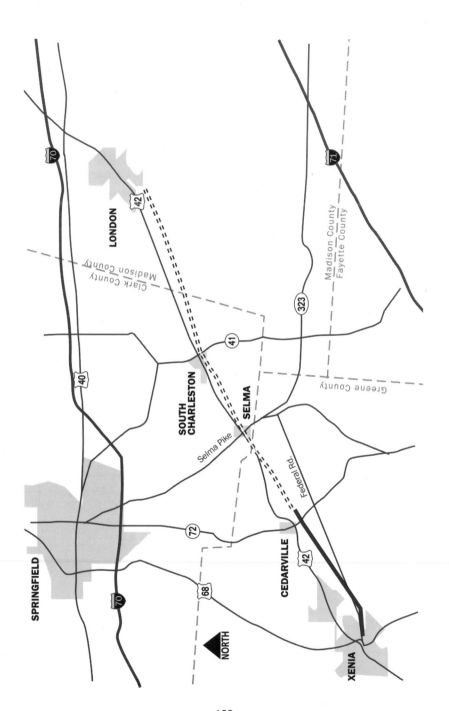

Little Miami Scenic Trail

Trail Uses	🚲 🏃 🛼 🏃 🔌
Area	Cincinnati, Springfield, Xenia
Trail Length	70 miles
Surface	Asphalt

Trail Notes

The Little Miami Scenic Trail was dedicated in 1999. This multi-use trail serves as a segment of the Ohio to Erie Trail System, and is designated as a part of the state-wide Buckeye Trail and the North Country National Scenic Trail. The Little Miami Scenic Trail travels from Milford northeast through Xenia and Yellow Springs to Springfield. In Springfield it merges with the Simon Kenton Trail. The Simon Kenton Trail then travels north about 20 miles to Urbana, in Champaign County. Clark, Greene, Warren, Clermont & Hamilton Counties each contain sections of the Little Miami Scenic Trail. Portions of the trail parallel the Little Miami River for which it was named. There are mile markers every ½ mile between Springfield and Xenia. The setting along your route includes rolling hills, farm country, deep gorges, small cliffs and outcroppings.

Trail Sections	Miles	Parking and rest room locations
Springfield to Yellow Springs	7.0	Yellow Springs
Yellow Springs to Xenia	9.7	Oldtown
Xenia to Spring Valley	7.2	Xenia
Spring Valley to Corwin	7.1	Spring Valley
Corwin to Morrow	14.7	Corwin
Morrow to Loveland	13.5	Caesar Creek State Canoe Access
Loveland to Milford	9.5	Fort Ancient State Memorial
Milford to Lunken Airport (under construction)	8.8	Kings Mills (Glenn Island State Canoe Access)
		Warren/Hamilton County Line
		Milford

Getting There

Northern Trailhead – I-70 one half mile south of John's Street in Springfield.

Southern Trailhead – Just north of OH-28, west of the Little Miami River.

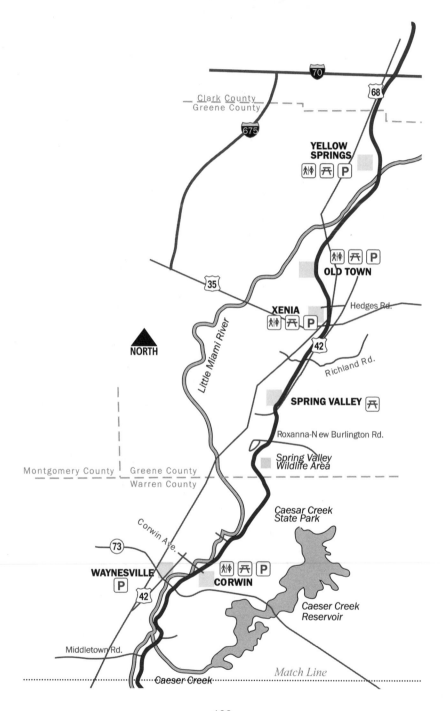

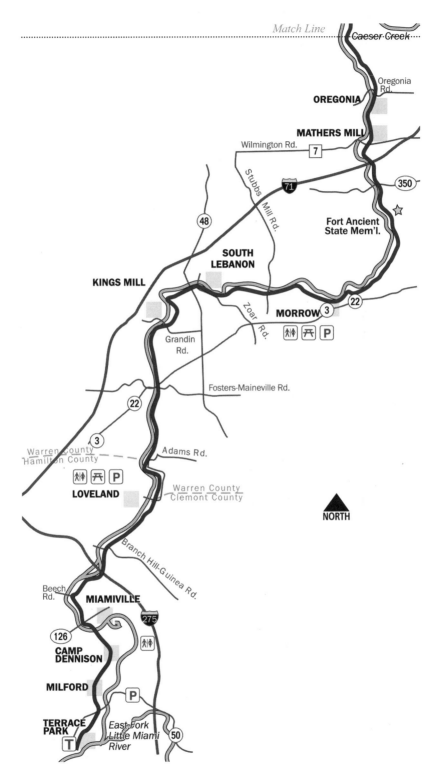

Caeser Creek

Oregonia Rd.

OREGONIA

MATHERS MILL

Wilmington Rd.
7

Stubbs Mill Rd.

71

350

48

Fort Ancient State Mem'l.

SOUTH LEBANON

KINGS MILL

Zoar Rd.

MORROW 3

22

Grandin Rd.

Fosters-Maineville Rd.

22

3

Warren County
Hamilton County

LOVELAND

Adams Rd.

Warren County
Clemont County

NORTH

Branch Hill-Guinea Rd.

Beech Rd.

MIAMIVILLE

275

126

CAMP DENNISON

MILFORD

P

TERRACE PARK
T

East Fork Little Miami River

50

Ohio to Erie Trail
Little Miami Scenic Trail (continued)

SPRINGFIELD

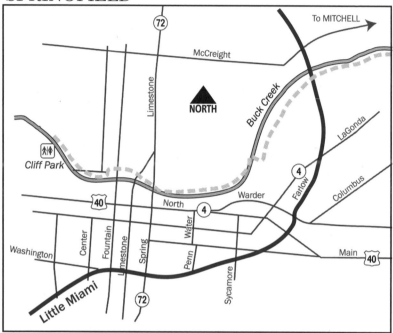

XENIA

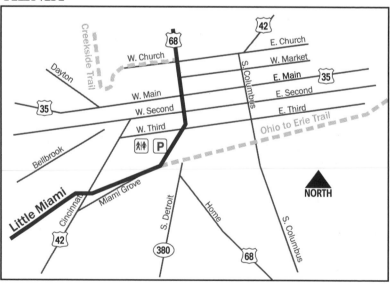

Olentangy-Scioto Bikeway

Trail Uses   🚲 🏃 ⛸

Area   Columbus

Trail Length   20 miles

Surface   Asphalt, concrete

Trail Notes

The Olentangy-Scioto Bikeway started out at 1.5 miles as Ohio's first rail-trail in 1967. The current trail starts at Frank Road and heads north, passing through Berliner Park, along the edge of German Village, and on through downtown Columbus and the OSU campus. Continuing northward it passes through several parks before ending at Worthington Hills Park. Future extensions will likely include a connector to the Ohio-to-Erie Trail as it makes its way to the nearby Alum Creek Bikeway, which lies to the east.

The trail continues to be updated and is generally in good condition, but there are some sharp corners and congested areas. There are a few bike route signs, but if you're unfamiliar with the area, the city streets and connecting paths can be confusing. The surface varies from asphalt to concrete, which includes some sidewalks. There are restroom and water facilities at the many parks along the trail. Suggested food stop include German Village, the downtown area, or the Short North areas.

Getting There

South End – The southern endpoint is at Frank Road, with nearby parking at Berliner Park behind the sports complex. Take Route 72 south or Route 70, Greenlawn Avenue exit and turn left. Then right on Deckenbach Road to the park's entrance and then left on Stimmel. Stimmel takes you around the sports complex to a parking lot. The trail is approximately .8 miles south of the parking lot. Look for a tree line on top of a small hill. Take note that the bikeway follows the edge of Berliner Park north to Greenlawn where you cross the river on the street bridge.

North End – The parking lot in the park off the East Wilson Bridge Road connects to an asphalt path that winds part the tennis courts and toward the river. This is the bikeway. The general rule is to stay on the path closest to the river whenever possible, heading south, as there are many connecting paths you'll encounter in the park.

Olentangy-Scioto Bikeway (continued)

Contact

Columbus Recreation and Parks Dept.   614-645-3308
200 Greenlawn Avenue
Columbus OH 43223

Access Points

Wilson Bridge Road

Whitney Avenue

Tucker Drive

Dubin-Granville Road (SR16)

Antrim Lake Park

Henderson Road

Bike/Pad Bridge (Markview Road)

Whetstone & Park of Roses (Ceramic Drive, Acton Road)

Northmoor Park (Orchard Lane)

Streets around East North Broadway

Clinton Como Park (Como Avenue, Pacemont Avenue, Weber Road)

Dodridge Street

Lower Scioto Multi-Use Trail

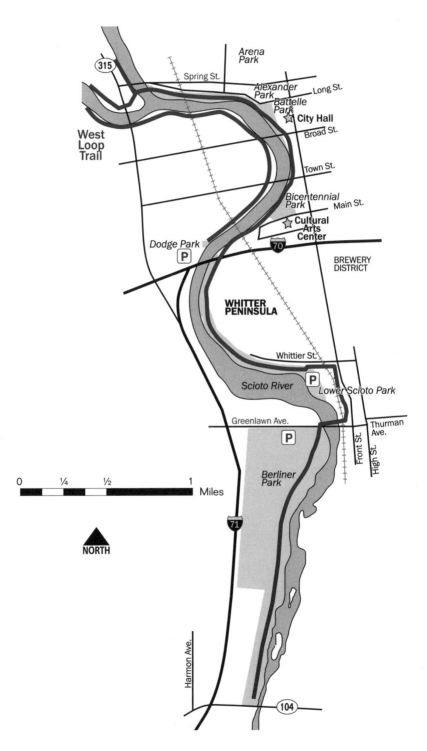

Arena Park

315

Spring St.

Alexander Park

Long St.

Battelle Park

☆ City Hall

Broad St.

West Loop Trail

Town St.

Bicentennial Park

Main St.

☆ Cultural Arts Center

Dodge Park

P

70

BREWERY DISTRICT

WHITTER PENINSULA

Whittier St.

P

Scioto River

Lower Scioto Park

Greenlawn Ave.

Thurman Ave.

P

Front St.

High St.

0 ¼ ½ 1

Miles

Berliner Park

71

▲ NORTH

Harmon Ave.

104

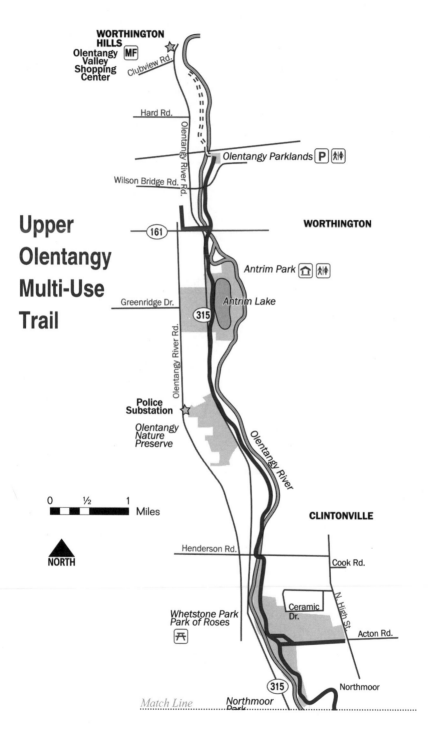

WORTHINGTON HILLS
Olentangy Valley Shopping Center MF

Clubview Rd.

Hard Rd.

Olentangy River Rd.

Olentangy Parklands P

Wilson Bridge Rd.

WORTHINGTON

161

Upper Olentangy Multi-Use Trail

Antrim Park

Antrim Lake

Greenridge Dr.

315

Olentangy River Rd.

Police Substation

Olentangy Nature Preserve

Olentangy River

0   ½   1
Miles

NORTH

CLINTONVILLE

Henderson Rd.

Cook Rd.

Ceramic Dr.

N. High St.

Acton Rd.

Whetstone Park Park of Roses

315

Northmoor

Match Line

Northmoor Park

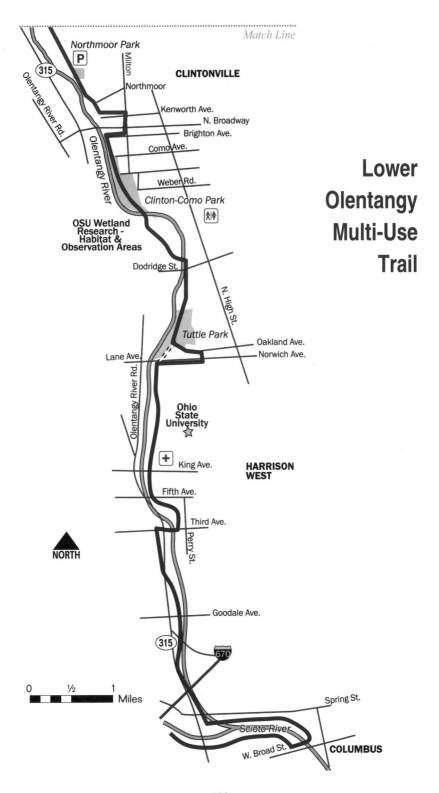

Match Line

Northmoor Park

P

315

CLINTONVILLE

Milton

Northmoor

Olentangy River Rd.

Kenworth Ave.

N. Broadway

Brighton Ave.

Olentangy River

Como Ave.

Lower
Olentangy
Multi-Use
Trail

Weber Rd.

Clinton-Como Park

OSU Wetland
Research -
Habitat &
Observation Areas

Dodridge St.

N. High St.

Tuttle Park

Oakland Ave.

Norwich Ave.

Lane Ave.

Olentangy River Rd.

Ohio
State
University

King Ave.

HARRISON
WEST

Fifth Ave.

Third Ave.

Perry St.

NORTH

Goodale Ave.

315

670

0   ½   1
Miles

Spring St.

Scioto River

W. Broad St.

COLUMBUS

Paint Creek State Park

Trail Uses	🚵 🏃 🧗
Area	Cincinnati
Trail Length	12 miles
Surface	Natural, groomed

Trail Notes

Paint Creek is located in Paint Creek Valley, and features a large lake. The park has a north and a south mountain biking loop. Both are mostly singletrack, and are well marked . The north loop has some technical terrain and a few hills, while the south loop is relatively flat and smooth. The trails pass through open meadows and mature woodlands.

Among the other activities available are camping, a 1,000 foot sand beach for swimming, boating, and rock climbing. A special feature of the park are the Seven Caves, all located 50 feet above Rocky Fork Creek. If you can spare the time, a short trip to the caves from the park are well worth your effort. The region lies at the edge of the Appalachian Plateau, which marks the boundary between the hilly eastern section and the flatter western portions of the state.

Getting There

From Cincinnati take US 50 about 15 miles past the town of Hillsboro to Rapid Forge Road just past the park entrance. At Rapid Forge Road take a left and follow it to Taylor Road. Go left and continue to the parking lot on the right side of the road, which is near the trail.

Contact

Paint Creek State Park   937-365-1401
14265 US Route 50
Bainbridge, Ohio 45612

TRAIL LEGEND	
────────	Trail-Biking/Multi
··············	Hiking only Trail
••••••••••	Hiking - Multi Use
▬▬▬▬▬▬	Snowmobiling only
==========	Planned Trail
▬ ▬ ▬ ▬ ▬	Alternate Trail
────────	Road/Highway
+++++++++++	Railroad Tracks

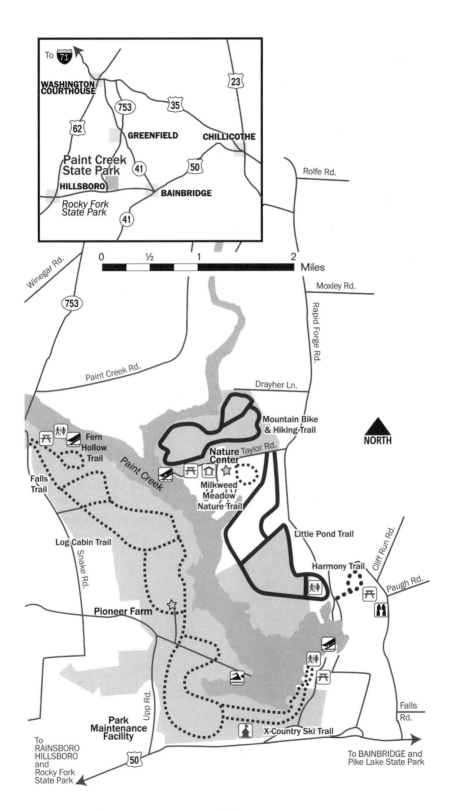

Pike State Forest

Trail Uses   🚵 🏃 🐴

Area   Chillicothe

Trail Length   38 miles

Surface   Natural, groomed

Trail Notes

Pike State Forest covers over 12,000 acres in western Pike County and eastern Highland County in southern Ohio. There are some 38 miles of bridle trail, which are shared with mountain bikers and hikers. Beautiful scenery and challenging terrain greet you as you wind through the forest hills and valleys. There are also numerous county and township roads that pass through the forest. Hiking is available on the Buckeye Trail.

Dense forests of oak, hickory, tulip, ash and other hardwoods characterize the Pike Lake region. In the springtime, the red bud and flowering dogwood trees provide spectacular displays of color, and wildflowers blanket the forest floor. During the fall, the hills come alive again with a panorama of vivid colors. Pike Lake State Park, located in the middle of Pike Forest, has a variety of recreational facilities such as camping, cabins, swimming, and boat rentals.

Getting There

To get to the Forest from Chillicothe, proceed south on US 23 past Waverly to SR 124. Head west on SR 124 to C-3. Proceed northwest for about 3 miles to the small community of Morgantown. From there you have a choice of continuing to any of several parking areas from which to begin your ride. See the map for parking locations.

Contact:

Pike Lake Forest   877-247-8733
1847 Pike Lake Road
Bainbridge, OH 45612

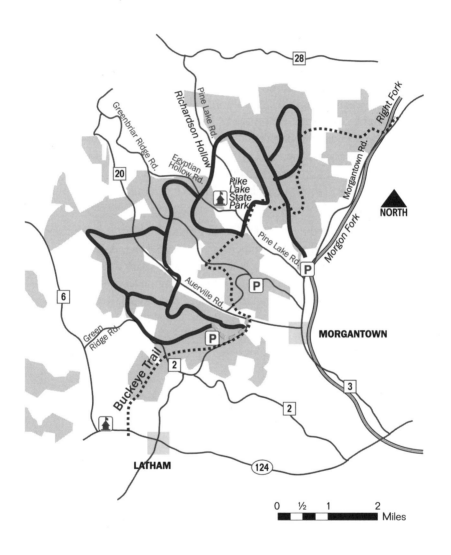

Richland B&O Trail

Trail Uses   🚴 🏃 🛼 🎿

Area	Mansfield
Trail Length	18.4 miles
Surface	Asphalt

Trail Notes

This multi-use trail was built on the rail bed of the former Baltimore & Ohio Railway. It's primarily a rural trail connecting the communities of Mansfield, Lexington, Bellville and Butler. The trail traverses some of the most scenic parts of North Central Ohio, from open farmlands, woods, and river crossings to short sections alongside a factory and mill. There are mile markers, occasional benches and parking areas along the route. The break stations in Bellville and Lexington also provide drink vending machines.

Leaving Mansfield, the trail begins some slight climbs as it passes under a few city street bridges until you cross Millsboro Road. As you head south, the trail passes Deer Park and alternates between tree cover and open countryside. Just past Main Street in Lexington (Route 42) is a bike shop on your right, should you have the need for service. Rentals are also available. Use caution when crossing Route 13 (Main Street) in Bellville, as the nearby bridge can obstruct your view of southbound traffic. As you approach Butler, you'll pass a local campground and lumber yard.

Getting There

The trailhead in Mansfield is located off the northwest corner of North Lake Park. In Butler the trailhead is located in Hitchman Park, off Elm Street.

Contact

Richland County Park District   419-884-3764
2295 Lexington Avenue
Mansfield, OH 44907

Distances

Mansfield to Lexington .... 7 miles

Lexington to Bellville .... 6 miles

Bellville to Butler .... 5 miles

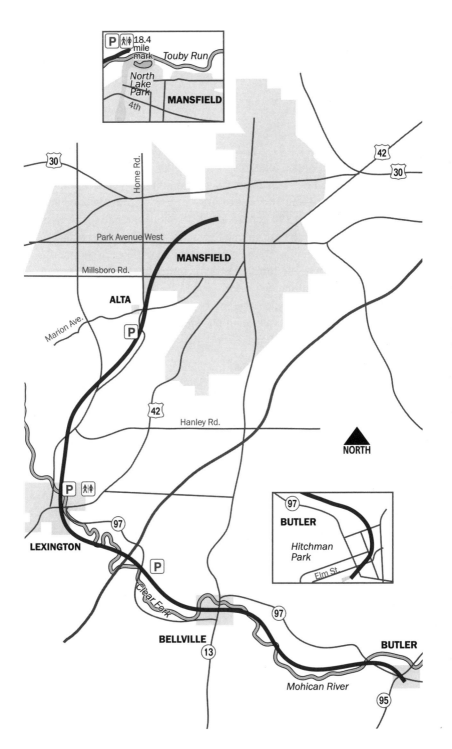

Scioto Trail State Forest

Trail Uses 🚵 🚶 🎧

Area   Chillicothe

Trail Length   26 miles

Surface   Natural

Trail Notes

Scioto Trail State Forest maintains over 26 miles of bridle trails for day use by mountain bikers, horseback riders and hikers. There are some 6 miles of paved roads and 18 miles of gravel roads to provide good access to all the areas in this 9,390 acre forest. Attractions include scenic vistas and overlooks, especially during the fall when the leaves are turning color. There is a Mountain Bike Family Campout held each summer to promote this activity. The forest was named after the Native American trail that ran from Chillicothe to Portsmouth. Route 23 follows the path of the trail. Facilities include a wading beach, camper cabins, a summer playground, picnic areas, water, and pit latrines.

Getting There

Access to the bridle trails is located off US 23, 9 miles south of Chillicothe. If you're coming from Chillicothe, watch for signs and take a left when you come to SR 372. This entrance takes you to the forest office area. See the illustrated map on the next page to select the road to get to your trailhead of choice.

Contact

Scioto Trail State Forest   740-663-2523
124 North Ridge Road
Waverly, Ohio 44690

SYMBOL LEGEND			
🏖	Beach/Swimming	MF	Multi-Facilities
🔧	Bicycle Repair	P	Parking
🏚	Cabin	🎍	Picnic
▲	Camping	🛖	Ranger Station
🛶	Canoe Launch	🚻	Restrooms
+	First Aid	🏠	Shelter
⦾	Food	T	Trailhead
GC	Golf Course	🏛	Visitor Center
?	Information	💧	Water
🛏	Lodging	🔭	Overlook/Observation

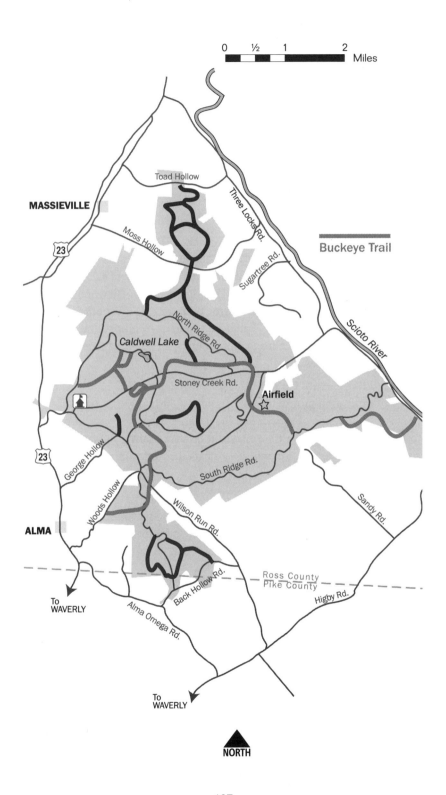

0   ½   1   2
Miles

Toad Hollow

MASSIEVILLE

Three Locks Rd.

Moss Hollow

23

Sugartree Rd.

Buckeye Trail

Scioto River

North Ridge Rd.

Caldwell Lake

Stoney Creek Rd.

Airfield

23

George Hollow

South Ridge Rd.

Sandy Rd.

Woods Hollow

ALMA

Wilson Run Rd.

Ross County
Pike County

To
WAVERLY

Back Hollow Rd.

Higby Rd.

Alma Omega Rd.

To
WAVERLY

▲
NORTH

137

Shaker Trace Trail
(Miami Whitewater Forest)

Trail Uses   🚲 🏃 ⛸ 🎧

Area	Cincinnati
Trail Length	9 miles
Surface	Asphalt

Trail Notes

The Shaker Trace Trail in Miami Whitewater Forest has a 7.8 mile outer loop and a 1.2 mile inner loop. The inner loop has 18 accessible Parcours fitness stations. Miami Whitewater Forest spans 4,279 acres and is located west of Cincinnati in Hamilton County. Bike and inline skate rentals are available at the Miami Whitewater Forest boathouses in addition to rowboats, pedal boats, and canoes. Additional facilities include an 18-hole golf course, campgrounds, an 85 acre fishing lake, and a soccer complex.

The Hamilton County Park District has been aggressively converting former farmland to prairie habitat. There is a 50 foot buffer of prairie plants on either side of the Shaker Trace Trail. Sometimes its hard to focus on biking with all the beautiful flowers nearby, such as the stiff goldenrod, compass plants, grey-headed cornflower and the royal catchfly.

Getting There

From I-74 exit on Dry Fork Road (Exit 3) and go north for 2 miles to Mt. Hope Road. At Mt. Hope Road take a right and go 1 mile to the Miami Whitewater Forest entrance and parking.

Contact

Miami Whitewater Forest Visitors Center 513-367-4774
9001 Mount Hope Road
Cincinnati, OH 45030

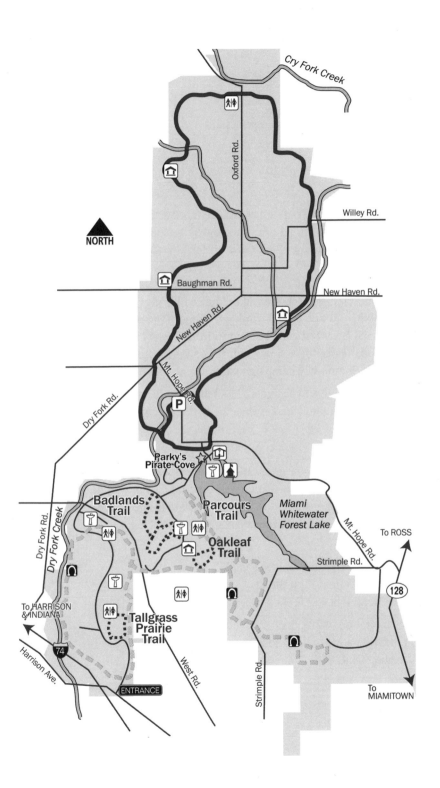

NORTH

Cry Fork Creek

Oxford Rd.

Willey Rd.

Baughman Rd.

New Haven Rd.

New Haven Rd.

Mt. Hope Rd.

Dry Fork Rd.

P

Parky's
Pirate Cove

Badlands
Trail

Parcours
Trail

Miami
Whitewater
Forest Lake

Oakleaf
Trail

Strimple Rd.

Dry Fork Rd.

Dry Fork Creek

To HARRISON
& INDIANA

Tallgrass
Prairie
Trail

74

Harrison Ave.

West Rd.

Strimple Rd.

Mt. Hope Rd.

To ROSS

128

To
MIAMITOWN

ENTRANCE

Simon Kenton Trail

Trail Uses	🚲 🏃 ⛸
Area	Urbana, Springfield
Trail Length	16.6 miles
Surface	Asphalt

Trail Notes

The Simon Kenton Trail will eventually connect to the Little Miami Scenic Trail at the corner of Center and Jefferson in downtown Springfield close to the Clark County Heritage Center. It will bypass downtown Springfield as it heads north and intersects its current southern terminus at the Buck Creek Trail immediately behind the Carleton Davidson Stadium. It crosses an old railroad bridge across Buck Creek, north on the rail line past North High School. The trail runs parallel to, and west of US 68. It continues north from County Line Road, passes under Cedar Bog Road at Woodburn Road, goes under SR 55, continues to Urbana Station in Champaign County and ends at Melvin Miller Park.

The trail is scenic and secluded. In Clark County it is shaded and is mostly below grade, whereas the trail in Champaign County runs by farm fields sunny with little shade. Rest rooms are available at Urbana Station.

Getting There

You can find park and ride locations at the Buck Creek Trail, Villa Road Stating Area just south of Villa Road East side, County Line Road, Woodburn Road just next to Cedar Bog, State Route 55 near Urbana, Urbana Station, and the Urbana YMCA.

Contact

Springfield Parks and Recreation 937-324-7348
City Hall, 76 East High Street
Springfield, OH 45502

Simon Kenton Pathfinders   837-484-4707
3420 Urbana-Moorefield Pike
Urbana, OH 43078

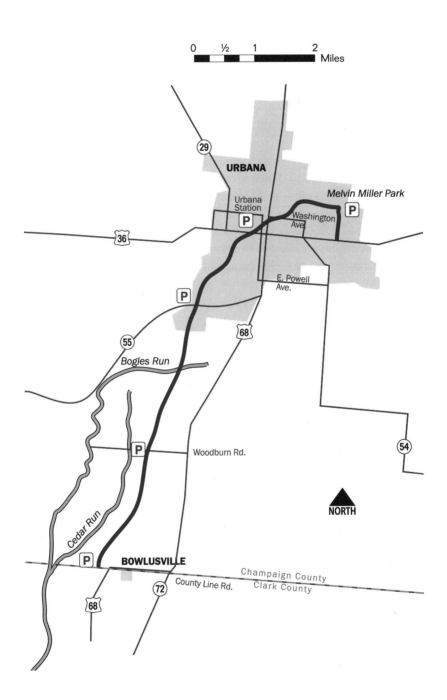

0   ½   1   2
                Miles

29

URBANA

Urbana
Station   *Melvin Miller Park*
            P   Washington   P
                       Ave.

36

E. Powell
Ave.

P

68

55

Bogles Run

P   Woodburn Rd.

▲
NORTH

54

Cedar Run

P   **BOWLUSVILLE**
                                    Champaign County
                        County Line Rd.   Clark County
68   72

Sippo Valley Trail

Trail Uses	🚴 🏃 🛼 🏃 𝐐
Area	Massillon
Trail Length	9.5 miles
Surface	Asphalt, limestone screenings

Trail Notes

This east-west, 9.5 mile park corridor in northeast Ohio links the downtowns of Dalton in Wayne County to Massillon in Stark County. It connects with the north-south Ohio-Erie Canal Towpath Trail by a combination of side streets signed as the "Discover Massillon" trail. The trail surface is asphalt at both the Dalton and Massillon ends while the middle three miles are crushed limestone. It is open every day from dawn to dusk. The equestrian trail is on a dirt path alongside the paved sections and jointly shared on the crushed limestone sections. There are trail markers every ½ mile. The trail takes its name from the nearby Sippo Creek and the small village of Sippo.

The Dalton trailhead is located at Village Green Park just east of the downtown and then joins the former rail line at the northeast edge of town. The route takes you through farmland settings, with grazing animals, pastureland, grain fields, and woodlots with plant and animal wildlife, meandering streams, wetlands, and rocky valleys as it approaches Bottoms Park and the Tuscarawas River in Massillon. The trail runs east to the river from Bottoms Park, then south under the Lincoln Way and Tremont Bridges and along a few city streets to Oak Knoll Park and onto Walnut Street and the Tuscarawas River Dike. Few remnants of a railroad remain other than some large metal signs with 8, 9, 12, and 16 on them, which served as mile markers from the Orrville Junction via Burton City and Dalton. You'll also see a wide concrete post with a large letter W, which was to signal engineers to blow the loud train whistle.

Getting There

The Dalton trailhead is located in Village Green Park, just south of Route 94 and east of I-30. The Massillon trailhead is located in Bottoms Parks, just north of 6th Street NW and Lincolnway (Route 172).

Contact

Stark County Park District   330-477-3552
5300 Tyner Street NW
Canton, Ohio 44708

AREA LEGEND

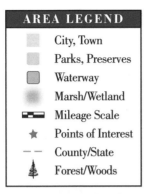

City, Town
Parks, Preserves
Waterway
Marsh/Wetland
Mileage Scale
★ Points of Interest
– – County/State
🌲 Forest/Woods

TRAIL LEGEND

———————— Trail-Biking/Multi
················· Hiking only Trail
•••••••••••• Hiking - Multi Use
▬▬▬▬▬▬ Snowmobiling only
========= Planned Trail
▬ ▬ ▬ ▬ ▬ ▬ Alternate Trail
———————— Road/Highway
++++++++++++ Railroad Tracks

SYMBOL LEGEND

🏊 Beach/Swimming
🚲 Bicycle Repair
🏠 Cabin
⬛ Camping
🛶 Canoe Launch
➕ First Aid
🅾 Food
⛳ Golf Course
❓ Information
🛏 Lodging
MF Multi-Facilities
P Parking
🍽 Picnic
🚶 Ranger Station
🚻 Restrooms
🏠 Shelter
T Trailhead
🏛 Visitor Center
🚰 Water
🔭 Overlook/
Observation

Courtesy of the Stark County Park District

Sippo Valley Trail (continued)

Courtesy of the Stark County Park District

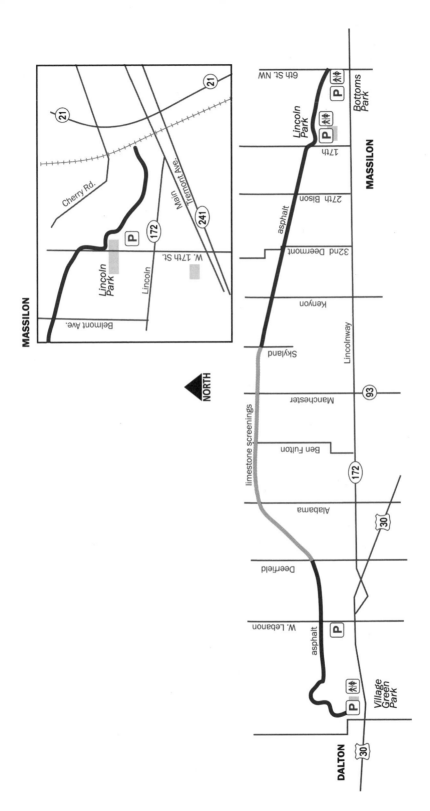

NORTH

MASSILON

6th St. NW
Lincoln Park
17th
Bottoms Park
MASSILON
27th Bison
asphalt
32nd Deermont
Kenyon
Lincolnway
Skyland
Manchester
limestone screenings
Ben Fulton
Alabama
Deerfield
W. Lebanon
asphalt
Village Green Park
DALTON

MASSILON
Cherry Rd.
Main Ave.
Tremont Ave.
W. 17th St.
Lincoln Park
Lincoln
Belmont Ave.

145

Slippery Elm Trail

Trail Uses	🚲 🏃 🛼 🎿 🐴
Area	Bowling Green, North Baltimore
Trail Length	13 miles
Surface	Asphalt, parallel equestrian dirt path

Trail Notes

The Slippery Elm Trail extends from Sand Ridge Road in Bowling Green, south through Rudolph, to East Broadway in North Baltimore. This multi-use trail is constructed on a former railway. The asphalt surface is 12 feet wide and is well maintained. Much of the trail is tree lined with frequent views of the surrounding countryside.

The trail does make a few street crossings heading out of North Baltimore to the open countryside. From there it makes several gradual "S" turns before straightening as it heads towards the village of Rudolf. From Rudolf it enters a section of woods and taller trees, then open fields. It continues underneath Hwy G before entering the north trailhead in the southwest corner of Bowling Green.

Parking with trail accesses

North trailhead – Sand Ridge Road at the Montessori School.

Portage Road, at the northeast corner of the trail intersection.

Rudolph Savanna Trail Access Ranger Station & grass parking area.

South trailhead – East Broadway in North Baltimore

Contact

Wood County Park District   419-353-1897

18729 Mercer Road, Bowling Green, Ohio 43402

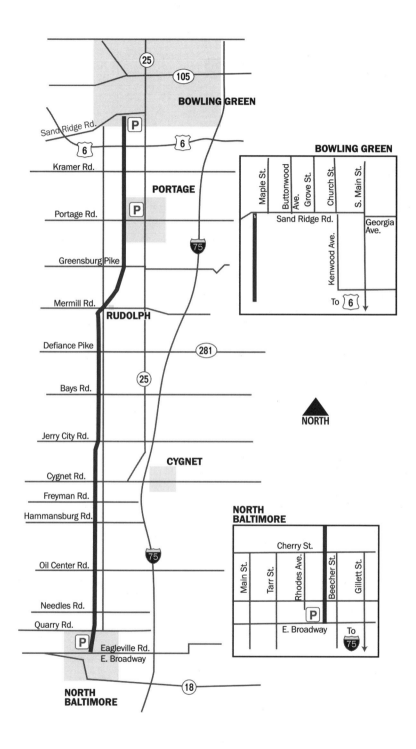

25

105

BOWLING GREEN

BOWLING GREEN

Sand Ridge Rd.

P

6   6

Kramer Rd.

Maple St.
Buttonwood Ave.
Grove St.
Church St.
S. Main St.

PORTAGE

P

Sand Ridge Rd.

Georgia Ave.

Portage Rd.

Kenwood Ave.

75

Greensburg Pike

Mermill Rd.

To 6

RUDOLPH

Defiance Pike

281

25

Bays Rd.

▲
NORTH

Jerry City Rd.

CYGNET

Cygnet Rd.

Freyman Rd.

Hammansburg Rd.

**NORTH
BALTIMORE**

Cherry St.

75

Main St.
Tarr St.
Rhodes Ave.
Beecher St.
Gillett St.

Oil Center Rd.

Needles Rd.

P

Quarry Rd.

P   Eagleville Rd.

E. Broadway

E. Broadway

To 75

**NORTH
BALTIMORE**

18

Stavich Bicycle Trail

Trail Uses   🚲 🏃 🛼 🎿

Area   Lowellville

Trail Length   11 miles

Surface   Asphalt

Trail Notes

The Stavich trail begins just west of Lowellville, Ohio and briefly follows Route 289 east into town. The trail is built on a former inter-urban electric rail route that parallels active train tracks. The tracks remains on fairly flat terrain while the bike trail climbs and descends during its entire length. This rising and falling will give you a good workout and a perspective that ranges from below railroad grade to far above where the tracks and a river are viewed from a good height. In two areas the trail surface ends and turns into street. Just continue in the same direction until the trail resumes again. A couple of the bridges have rough wooden surfaces, and can even be a bit dangerous at high speeds.

The trail, constructed and maintained by the families of John and George Stavich, follows the Mahoning River from Struthers, Ohio, to New Castle, Pennsylvania, offering users a vast variety of scenery, including green rolling hills, farmlands, and wooded hillsides. The 11 mile bicycle trail has an 8 foot wide asphalt surface. There are benches along the route and a picnic area near the trailhead in Pennsylvania. Food and water is available in the communities along the route.

Getting There

Trailheads are located in Lowellville and Struthers, Ohio, and in New Castle and Edinburg, Pennsylvania. Parking can be found along Liberty Street in Lowellville where the trail runs for seven blocks. Parking is also available in New Castle, PA on Washington Street.

Lawrence County Tourism Bureau   724-536-8408
228 Jefferson Street
New Castle, PA 16101

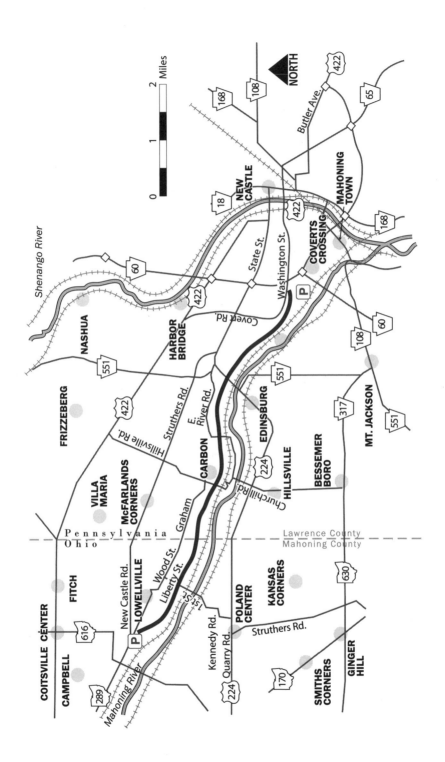

149

Stonelick State Park

Trail Uses   🚵 🥾

Area	Cincinnati
Trail Length	5.3 miles
Surface	Natural, groomed

Trail Notes

Stonelick State Park is located in rural Clermont County in the highlands of southwest Ohio, 22 miles from Cincinnati. The park offers a quiet retreat with the still waters of the lake and unusual stands of mature sweet gum trees, uncommon wildflowers and abundant fossils. The 5.3 miles of trail are open to hiking and mountain bikes.

Several Lakeside and wooded picnic area have tables and grills. The 200 acre Stonelick Lake offers a sand beach. Boat rentals are available. There are over 100 campsites, most of which have electricity. The campground is also equipped with showers, flush toilets, a dump station, a camp store and laundry facilities. The park site sits in the Cincinnati Arch, formed during the time the Appalachian Mountains were formed. The rocks of the arch contain so many fossils of diverse species that they have become very famous and continue to attract visitors to the park.

Getting There

From Cincinnati take Hwy 50 northeast to SR 131, then east on SR 131 to SR 727. Take SR 727 northeast, a quarter mile past Newtonville Road to the trailhead and parking area on your left.

Contact

Stonelick State Park   513-734-4323
2895 Lake Drive
Pleasant Plain, Ohio 45162

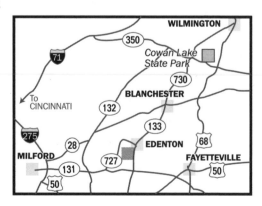

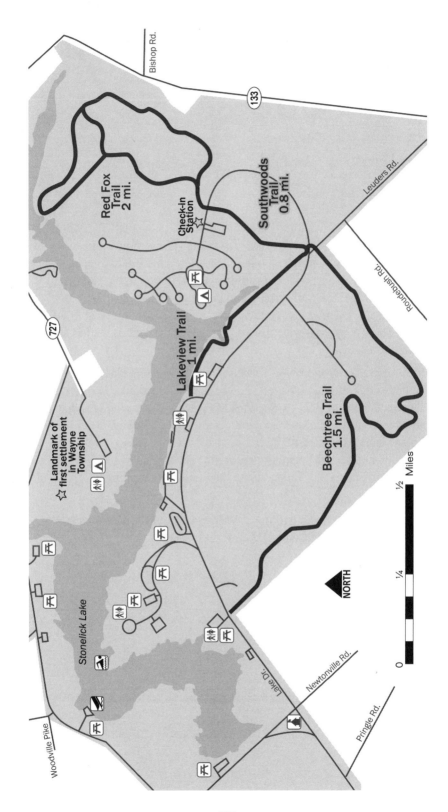

Bishop Rd.

133

Leuders Rd.

Roudebush Rd.

Red Fox Trail 2 mi.

Check-in Station

Southwoods Trail/ 0.8 mi.

727

Lakeview Trail 1 mi.

Beechtree Trail 1.5 mi.

Landmark of first settlement in Wayne Township

Stonelick Lake

Woodville Pike

Lake Dr.

Newtonville Rd.

Pringle Rd.

NORTH

0   ¼   ½   Miles

151

University Parks Bike-Hike Trail

Trail Uses 🚵 🏃 👟

Area	Toledo
Trail Length	6.3 miles
Surface	Asphalt

Trail Notes

This level, 12 foot wide trail stretches from the University of Toledo campus to King Road in Sylvania Township. The setting is a lush greenway passing through woodland, meadows and wetlands. There are several neighborhood access points, a connection to the Wildwood Preserve Metropark trail system, and designated roadway connections to Ottawa Park, Olander Park, and the Westfield Shoppingtown at Franklin Park. There is a 6 foot wide, paved loop inside the park as well as some hiking trials.

Most of the University Parks Trail has fencing running alongside, even on both sides at times. The fencing varies from chain line, to split rail and wooden privacy fence. Sections of the trail pass through residential neighborhoods, and also a few commercial areas. The University of Toledo campus section has light posts, and railroad tracks parallel the trail at the edge of the campus. Restrooms are available in Wildwood Metro Park, and water fountains can be found in the campus.

Getting There

There is a trailhead and parking at Wildwood Preserve Metro Park. You can enter the park off Central Avenue east of I-475.

Contact

Metropark District of the Toledo Area   419-535-3050
5100 W. Central Avenue
Toledo, OH 43615

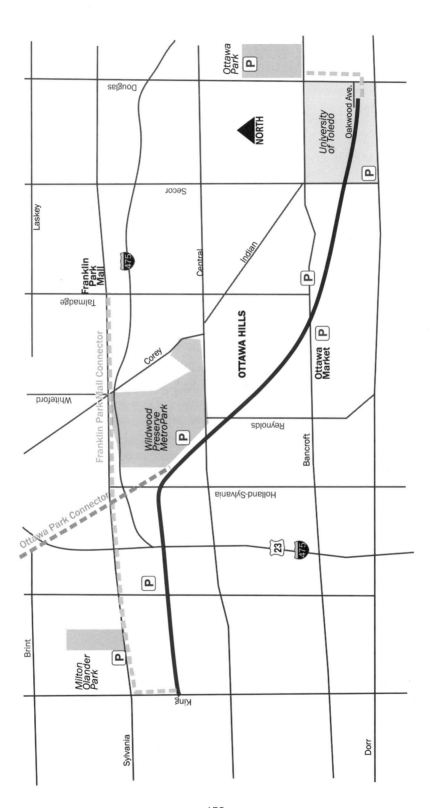

Van Buren State Park

Trail Uses   🚵 🥾 🏇

Area   Findley

Trail Length   6 miles

Surface   Natural, groomed

Trail Notes

The 6 miles of mountain bike trail are shared as hiking and bridle trails. Van Buren State Park is located in the rich agricultural plains of northwest Ohio. Beech and sugar maple occupy a large portion of the wooded area in the park. Wildflowers also abound in the fields and in these woodlands. Animals found in the area include red fox, raccoon, skunk, opossum, and while-tailed deer. There is a multi-use campground at the east end of the park, with tables, pit latrines, and a dump station. Rowboats, canoes, and boats with electric motors only are allowed on Van Buren Lake.

The region was originally inhabited by the Shawnee Indians, which were banished from their homeland in south-central Ohio. Eventually they departed for lands west of the Mississippi River. Indian artifacts and relics can still be found on what used be called Indian Island, located in the northwest section of the lake. The park was named for Martin Van Buren, eighth President of the United States.

Getting There

Van Buren is located just north of the town of Findlay. From Findlay take I-75 north to SR 613. Go east of SR 613 to TR 218. TR 218 heads south, then eastbound for a little over 2 miles before coming to TR 229. Take TR 229 south into the park. You will find parking on both sides of TR 229, and trails accesses on the east side of the road.

Contact

Van Buren State Park   419-832-7662
12259 Township Road 218
Van Buren, Ohio 45889

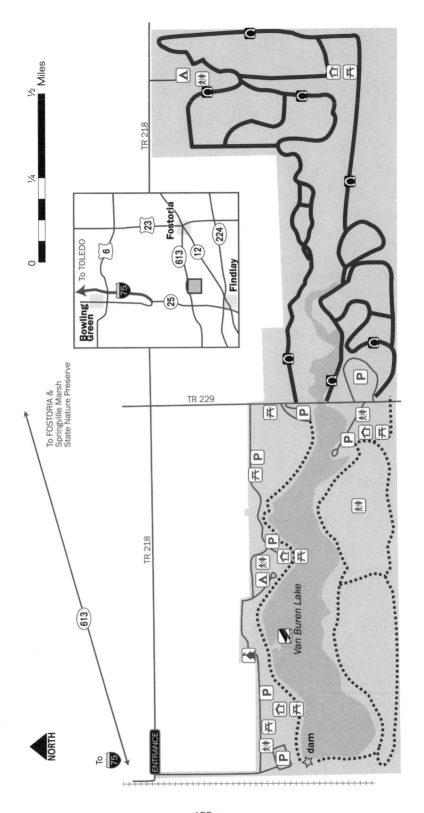

Vulture's Knob
Race Course

Trail Uses	🚵
Area	Wooster
Trail Length	7 miles
Surface	Natural

Trail Notes

This is a private property Pay-To-Ride trail, and is considered one of Ohio's top rated Mountain Bike Race Courses. The trails are open daily from May 1 through October 31, and weekends only from November 1 through April 30.

The original course is made up of a short, intense loop through wooded valleys, an old quarry, grassy hillsides and a small pine tree plantation. There are a few long climbs, and every downhill ends in a turn abrupt enough to kill your speed, followed by wearing pitched climbs. There are numerous log bridges. A second loop follows Killbuck Creek and its adjacent hillsides, and is more open than the original trail. It features a lot of flat twisting singletrack through a creek bottom. The trail is well marked.

Getting There

Vulture's Knob is located west of Wooster. From the south take I-71 north to US 30 east. Exit SR3 south but turn north (right) and then left on Liberty, which becomes Mechanicsburg Road. Follow the gravel road on your left at 4300 Mechanicsburg Road down past a house to the open barn. The trailhead and a map are at the barn. Coming from Cleveland you can take I-71 south to SR 3 or SR 83 south. Turn west (right) on Smithville Western Road and south (left) on Mechanicsburg Road.

Contact

Vulture's Knob Mountain Bike Race Course   330-264-7636
4300 Mechanicsburg Road
Wooster, Ohio 44691

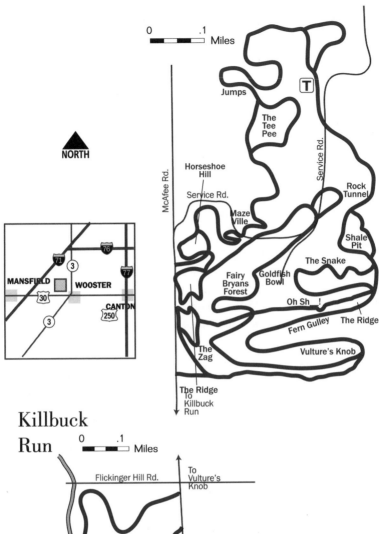

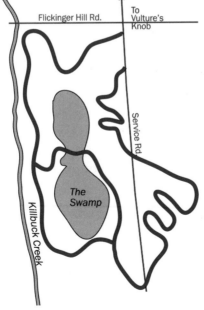

Wabash Cannonball Trail

Trail Uses	🚲 🚴 🏃 ⛷ 🎒
Area	Toledo
Trail Length	64 miles
	North fork, 46 miles (about 9 miles paved)
	South fork, 17 miles (about 10 miles paved)
Surface	Asphalt, cinder, undeveloped

Trail Notes

The Wabash Cannonball Trail is one of the longest in the state, stretching 64 miles through Lucas, Fulton, Henry and Williams Counties, and the Oak Openings, Ohio's most unique natural area. The trail follows two former rail lines forming a North and a South Fork, converging at Jerome Road in Maumee, near the Fallen Timbers Battlefield.

The North Fork runs east and west from Maumee to Montpeller, coming to within 15 miles of the Indiana state line. It is paved to the Lucas County border. There is also a paved connection linking with the 5.3 mile Oak Openings Preserve multi-use trail. The South Fork takes a southwesterly route, running from Maumee to the edge of Liberty Center. It passes through Maumee State Forest and the Village of Whitehouse. It is also paved to the Lucas County border. Where the paved sections of the trail end, the remainder is currently cinder based, suitable for mountain bikes and horses.

Nearby parking:

The best parking near the trail is currently at Oak Openings (Maumee State Forest in the Springbrook area) on SR64, or downtown Whitehouse. You'll also find parking along Jerome Road and Monclova Elementary School on Monclova Road.

Contact

Northwestern Ohio Rails-to-Trails Association   419-822-4788
PO Box 234
Delta, OH 43515

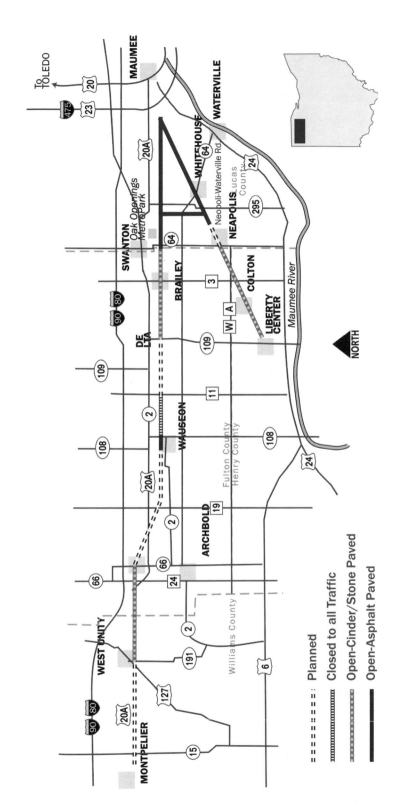

NORTH

Legend:
- ========== Planned
- ▦▦▦▦▦ Closed to all Traffic
- ▪▪▪▪▪ Open-Cinder/Stone Paved
- ━━━━━ Open-Asphalt Paved

Map labels: MAUMEE, To TOLEDO, WATERVILLE, WHITEHOUSE, NEAPOLIS, Neopoli-Waterville Rd, Lucas County, SWANTON, Oak Openings Metro Park, BRAILEY, COLTON, LIBERTY CENTER, Maumee River, DELTA, WAUSEON, Fulton County, Henry County, ARCHBOLD, WEST UNITY, MONTPELIER, Williams County

Route markers: 20, 23, 475, 20A, 64, 24, 295, 3, W, A, 109, 11, 108, 2, 90, 80, 66, 19, 24, 191, 6, 127, 15

West Branch State Park

Trail Uses   🚵 🚶 🎧 🐾

Area	Cleveland
Trail Length	9 miles
Surface	Natural, groomed

Trail Notes

The park is located in Portage County, about 5 miles east of Ravenna, and is Cleveland's closest legal and public mountain bike trail system, although the trails started as snowmobile trails. CAMBA has now bypassed most of these trails with singletrack tread. These trails are accessed by Cable Line Road, which allows only cyclists and hikers with loops to the north and south of it. Trails are bi-directional.

The lakeside portion of the trail is located on the north side of Cable Line Road and consists of flowing single-track that traces along the shore of the reservoir. This section of trail features many short climbs and descents in and out of the ravines that line the lake. You will also experience some large log piles, narrow log bridges, and many roots. This portion of the trail is easy to moderate, but some of the downhill sections may be more technical. The single-track on the south side of Cable Line Road is more technical and challenging. The "Rock Gorge Trail" provides some very scenic riding with singletrack that drop the rider into a gorge with a flowing creek below and also includes several very rocky sections. The "Rock Wall Trail" offers some extremely challenging rock riding. This section includes some tricky downhills and difficult climbs consisting entirely of large rocks.

Getting There

From Cleveland – take I-480 East, which become OH-14. From OH-14 turn left onto OH-59, which become OH-5. After several miles you'll come to Rock Spring Road on your right. Turn right onto Rock Spring Road.

From Akron/Canton – take I-77 South to the I-76 east exit at Route 5/44. Proceed on Route 5 east to Rock Spring Road and turn right.

Follow Rock Spring Road across the reservoir for less than a ½ mile, and you'll see signs for the mountain bike/snowmobile trails on the left side. Follow the road for a ¼ mile to trailhead parking on your right with a kiosk along the tree line.

Contact

West Branch State Park   330-296-3239
5708 Esworth Road
Ravenna, Ohio 44266

Point-to-Point Trail Directions courtesy of CAMBA

From parking lot:

Climb snowmobile trail exiting from back of Kiosk. (Pavement of Cable Line Rd. can be used to bypass this snowmobile trail when it is wet.)

Turn left onto Cable Line Rd. (Cable Line Rd. is the main road through our trails, it can be used as easy access to the trail network.)

Ride Cable Line Rd. for twenty yards.

Turn left onto singletrack "Lakeside Trail" for 1.77 miles.

On singletrack, cross snowmobile trail onto "F-loop bypass" for .1 mile.

On singletrack, cross snowmobile trail continuing on "F-loop bypass" for .36 mile.

Turn left onto snowmobile trail into dip and cross culvert.

Turn left onto E-loop snowmobile trail for approximately .5 mile.

Turn left onto singletrack "D-E-loop Connector" for .51 mile.

Turn left onto D-loop snowmobile trail.

After crossing wooden bridge turn left onto singletrack "Kitchen Sink" trail for approximately .5 mile.

Turn left onto D-loop snowmobile trail, look for an immediate right.

Turn right onto singletrack "D-loop bypass".

Cross D-loop snowmobile trail onto "End Loop" trail for .49 mile.

Turn left onto D-loop snowmobile trail.

Turn right onto Cable Line Rd.   Look for first snowmobile trail on left.

Turn left onto C-loop snowmobile trail for approximately .25 mile.   Look for right into singletrack "Gorge Trail".

Turn right onto "Gorge Trail" for 1.09 mile.

At end of "Gorge Trail" switchback left onto "Two Pond Trail" for about 1 mile. This trail is marked "More Difficult".

Beginners and Intermediate riders, turn left onto B-loop snowmobile trail for approximately 1 mile.

Beginners, Intermediates, go straight onto A-loop snowmobile trail for 1.06 mile.

Beginners, Intermediates, cross Cable Line Road. onto snowmobile trail to Kiosk and parking area.

Experts stay straight onto "Rockwall" trail.   This trail is marked with an "Experts Only" sign.

Experts turn left onto B-loop snowmobile trail and climb.   Look for trail marked "most difficult" on right two thirds of the way up the climb.

Experts turn right onto "Bit-O-Honey Trail".

Exit "Bit-O-Honey Trail" and diagonally cross snowmobile loop "B" onto "Brokeback Trail" it is marked "most difficult".   The entrance to "Brokeback Trail" is just below the exit of "Rockwall Trail".

"Brokeback Trail" crosses the snowmobile loop "A" once, and exits directly across from the entrance to "Lakeside Trail".

Experts turn left onto Cable Line Rd.

Go twenty yards and turn right onto snowmobile connector and ride down to Kiosk and parking area.

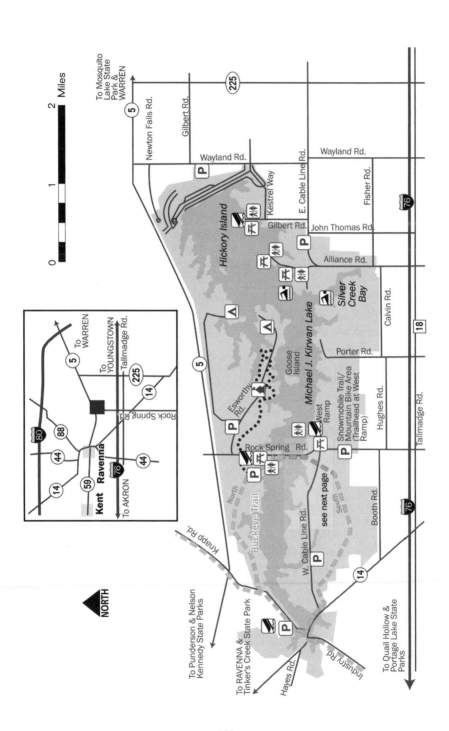

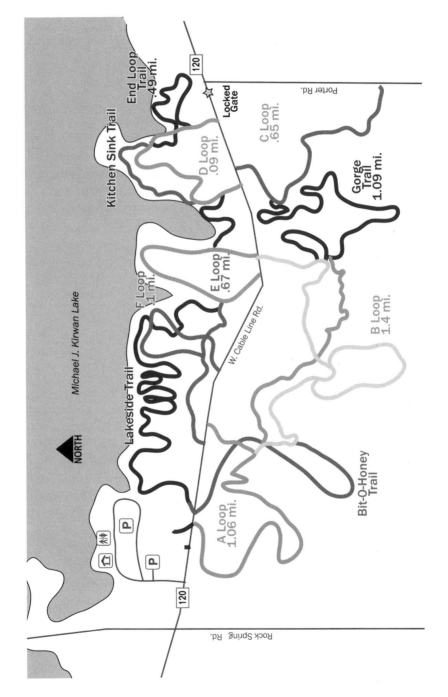

NORTH

Michael J. Kirwan Lake

Lakeside Trail

Kitchen Sink Trail

End Loop Trail .49 mi.

D Loop .09 mi.

C Loop .65 mi.

Locked Gate

Porter Rd.

120

Gorge Trail 1.09 mi.

F Loop .1 mi.

E Loop .67 mi.

W. Cable Line Rd.

B Loop 1.4 mi.

A Loop 1.06 mi.

Bit-O-Honey Trail

P

P

120

Rock Spring Rd.

Additional Trails

Black Creek Reservation

Trail Uses 🚲 🏃 🛼 ⛷️

Area	Elyria, Lorain
Trail Length	3.5 miles
Surface	Paved

Trail Notes

Known as the Bridgeway Trail, it follows the Black River between Elyria and Lorain in Lorain County. The trail passes through meadows and forest groves, under bridges and over treetops on a 1,000 foot bridge that crosses the river in two places. This bridge is the highlight of the trail, offering captivating views of the river, with shale cliffs on one side and an expanse of bottomlands on the other.

Contact

Black River Reservation 440-324-5481

Buck Creek Trail

Trail Uses 🚲 🏃 🛼 ⛷️

Area	Springfield
Trail Length	9 miles
Surface	Asphalt

Trail Notes

This is a beautifully wooded trail, which follows Buck Creek from Plum Street through Veteran's Park and then follows Warder Street to North Limestone Street to the Old Reid Park across Croft Road and into Buck Creek State Park. Parking and restrooms are available in Old Reid Park off Pumphouse and Croft Road, in Buck Creek State Park on Croft Road, and in the Buck Creek State Park beach parking lots. From Columbus take I-70 West to Route 40 (Exit 62). Go west for 3 miles to the first traffic light, and then right on North Bird Road to Buck Creek Lane. Total distance is about 48 miles.

Contact

Buck Creek State Park   937-322-5284

Celena to Coldwater Bike Trail

Trail Uses 🚲 🎿 🛼 🏃

Area	Coldwater
Trail Length	4.5 miles
Surface	Asphalt

Trail Notes

The south end of the trail ends at Vine and Fourth Streets in Coldwater. A couple of blocks east of the north trailhead is Grand Lake St. Marys. There is a parking lot and picnic area at the south end of the State Park, on the west side of the lake on West Band Road. Just north of the dam is Schumck Road, which leads to the north end of the trail.

Contact   City of Celina 419-586-1144

Greenway Corridor Bikeway

Trail Uses 🚲 🎿 🛼

Area	Painesville
Trail Length	4.5 miles
Surface	Asphalt

Trail Notes

The Bikeway trails the route once owned by the Baltimore and Ohio Railroad. The corridor links the municipalities of Painesville, Painesville Township and Concord Township. The elevation varies, ranging from 660 feet in Painesville to 895 feet in Concord Township.

Contact   Lake Metroparks   440-639-7275

Hamilton Bikeway

Trail Uses 🚲 🎿 🛼

Area	Hamilton
Trail Length	6 miles
Surface	Asphalt

Trail Notes

This 10 foot wide asphalt bikeway parallels the Great Miami River and winds through a nature preserve connecting the Soldiers, Sailors and Pioneers Monument near the center of Hamilton with Fairfield to the South. There are plans to extend the trail north to connect with trails traveling through Dayton. The Riverside Natural Area, with its 150 acres, is worth a side visit to enjoy its natural beauty. It's located adjacent to the path along the Great Miami River.

Contact   Hamilton City Parks   523-785-7060

Additional Trails (continued)

Headwaters Trail

Trail Uses

Area   Mantua

Trail Length   7 miles

Surface   Limestone screenings

Trail Notes

The trail is located in northern Portage County, and the setting for your ride is beautiful forest and farmland as it crosses the continental drainage divide. The western trailhead begins in Mantua at the Village Park on High Street and goes east to Asbury Road for a distance of a little over 3 miles. At that point there is a 1.5 mile gap. Follow the bike route signs along back roads to Hiram Station on SR-700. From there the trail continues east for another 3 miles to the Village Park Library in Garrettsville.

Contact

Portage Park District   330-297-7728

I-480 Bikeway

Trail Uses

Area   North Olmsted

Trail Length   6.5 miles

Surface   Asphalt

Trail Notes

The I-480 Bikeway follows the north side if I-480 between Great Northern Blvd. and Stearns Road.

Contact

City of North Olmsted   440-777-8000

Lester Rail Trail

Trail Uses   🚴 🚶 🛼

Area	Medina
Trail Length	3.2 miles
Surface	Asphalt

Trail Notes

This 3.2 mile biking/hiking trail runs from Abbeyville Road to Lester Road in York Township. The terrain is mostly level and travels through farmland and prairie remnants. There is parking at the rear of the Medina County Career Center in the northeast corner of the parking lot or on Lester Road.

Contact

Medina County Park District   330-722-9364

Lunken Airport Bike Path

Trail Uses   🚴 🚶 🛼 🎿

Area	Cincinnati
Trail Length	5.5 miles
Surface	Asphalt

Trail Notes

The bike path circles around Lunken Airport and will connect to the proposed extension of the Ohio to Erie Trail. The trail also goes around a golf course and along a children's playground. From the trail, across the Ohio River, you can see the Kentucky hillside where the Tower Park Trail is located. Parking is available in the park on Wilmer Avenue next to Beechmont Avenue. The is a fairly steep hill at the far side of the runway as it follows the Little Miami River.

Additional Trails (continued)

National Road Bikeway
Trail Uses

Area	St. Clairsville
Trail Length	4 miles
Surface	Asphalt

Trail Notes

This rail-trail runs north and south, crossing below I-70 and through a tunnel under US 40. This is Ohio's only rail-trail with a tunnel. The tunnel is 532 feet long and 40 feet high. There is interior lighting. The northern end of the tunnel features a two plaza overlook allowing the user an 80 foot high view of the bike trail at the top level.

Contact

St. Clairsville Recreation Dept.   740-695-2037

Nickelplate Trail
Trail Uses

Area	Louisville
Trail Length	2.5 miles
Surface	Asphalt

Trail Notes

This short trail runs underneath Nickelplate Street in Louisville. You can add more mileage to your ride by entering Metzger Park via connecting paths and riding the park loop there. There are benches and markers every half mile, but two of the benches have railroad ties installed in the trail surface to act as speed bumps. The scenery consists mostly of woods and meadows. Parking is available at the southeast entrance to the trail next to Dellbrook Avenue, and in Metzger Park off Nickelplate Avenue and south of Edmar Street.

Contact

Stark County Park District   330-477-3552

Oakwood Park

Trail Uses   🚵 🏃 👟

Area	Napoleon
Trail Length	3 miles
Surface	Natural

Trail Notes

This is a single-track trail made up of two loops. The climbs and descents are steep at times. Oakwood Park is near the intersection of Oakwood Avenue and Northcrest Drive in Napoleon.

Contact   Oakwood Park 418-592-4233

Piqua Linear Park

Trail Uses   🚵 🏃 👟

Area	Piqua
Trail Length	11 miles
Surface	Asphalt

Trail Notes

The initial phase of the trail runs east and west along an abandoned railroad bed through the center of the city, and is tree lined. Much of the next section completed runs along the hydraulic canal from French Park to Swift Run Lake north of the city. The last section of the Linear Park to be completed is designated "River's Edge", and runs from Swift Run Lake to Lock Nine Park, along the Great Miami River and follows the former Miami-Erie Canal in some places.

Contact   Piqua Parks & Recreation   937-778-2085

Westerville Bikeway

Trail Uses   🚵 🏃 👟

Area	Westerville
Trail Length	3 miles
Surface	Asphalt

Trail Notes

This rail-trail runs north from Cherrington Road to Maxtown Road. There are plans to connect this trail to Mt. Vernon and the Kokosing Gap Trail. The setting is urban and wooded areas.

Contact   Westerville Parks   614-890-8544

Additional Trails (continued)

Wright Brothers Bikeway

Trail Uses   🚲 🚶 ⛸️

Area	Dayton
Trail Length	4.7 miles
Surface	Asphalt & Concrete

Trail Notes

The Wright Brothers Bikeway was formerly known as the Huffman Prairie Overlook Trail and also as the Kauffman Avenue Bikeway. The bikeway runs from Fairborn to the Wright Brothers Memorial. Parking is available at the Memorial and in Eastwood Metropark.

Contact

Miami Valley Regional Bicycle Council   937-463-2707

Zanes Bikeway

Trail Uses   🚲 🚶 ⛸️

Area	Zanesville
Trail Length	3 miles
Surface	Asphalt

Trail Notes

The path follows the east bank of the Muskingum River from Market Street in downtown Zanesville to Riverview Park. The ride provides good views of the river, and you'll pass a restored train depot near the south entrance. There is a barrier separating the trail from the railroad still in use.

Contact

Zanesville Parks & Recreation Dept.   740-455-0609

Organizations

Bike Miami Valley
PO Box 246
Dayton, OH 45402
www.bikemiamivalley.org

Central Ohio Bicycle Advocacy Coalition
PO Box 2003
Columbus, OH 43216-2003
614-888-9866
www.cobac.org

Great Ohio Bicycle Adventure
1525 Bethel Road, Ste. 100
Columbus, OH 43220
614-273-0811
www.goba.com

Hostelling International – Toledo Area
PO Box 352736
Toledo, OH 43635-2736
www.freewheel.com

League of American Bicyclists
1612 K Street NW, Ste 800
Washington, DC 20006-2850
202-822-1333
www.bikeleague.org

Ohio Bicycle Federation
825 Olde Farm Court
Vandalia, OH 45377
937-656-0814
www.ohiobike.org

Ohio Dept. of Transportation
Distributes packets of information on Bicycling in Ohio and Bicycle Safety. Offers a brochure "Biking Ohio – Map and list of Bikeways in Ohio."
ODOT, Bicycle/Pedestrian Program
PO box 899
Columbus, OH 43216
614-644-7095

Ohio Rails-to-Trail Conservancy
Plays a leading role in converting Ohio's abandoned railroad corridors into trails for bicycling.
614-841-1075

Ohio Bicycle Clubs

Akron Bicycle Club
PO Box 2268
Stow, OH 44224-1000
Touring
http://akronbike.org

Arrupe Bicycle Club
Ohio City Bicycle Co-op
1823 Columbus Rd.
Cleveland, OH 44113-2411
Training
http://www.ohiocitycycles.org/

Ashtabula Ymca Bicycling Club
PO Box 28
Ashtabula, OH 44005-0028
Touring

Arrupe Bicycle Club
c/o Ohio City Bicycle Co-op
3404 Lorain Ave.
Cleveland, OH 44113-3704
Education/touring
http://www.ocbc.freewebsites.com/

Athens Bicycle Club
14 W Stimson Ave.
Athens, OH 45701
Touring/mtn
http://www.athensbicycleclub.org/
Info@athensbicycleclub.org

Athens Velo
104 W Union
Athens, OH 45701

Battelle Bicycle Club
505 King Ave.
Columbus, OH 43201-2693

Casual Cruisers
3159 Montana Ave.
Cincinnati, OH 45211-6734
Touring

Central Ohio Bicycle Club
c/o Breakaway Cycling
17 W William St.
Delaware, OH 43015
Racing   Teamcobc@aol.com
http://www.team-cobc.com/

Cincinnati Cycle Club
PO Box 43441
Cincinnati, OH 45243-0441
Touring
http://www.cincinnaticycleclub.org/

Cincinnati Velo Club
Glenn Wolf
241 W Mcmillan St
Cincinnati, OH 45219

Clark County Freewheelers
1774 S. Center Blvd.
Springfield, OH 45506-3154
Touring

Cleveland Area Mountain Bike Assoc.
http://www.joinomba.org/camba/

Cleveland Touring Club
PO Box 1157
Mentor, OH 44061
Touring
http://www.clevelandtourclub.org/
Clevetourclub@hotmail.com

Clintonville Cycling Club
Sara West
3517 Kinsale Head Dr
Columbus, OH 43221-4461
Touring
Sarawest@columbus.rr.com

Club Glenwood
Ted Schmidt
61 Savannah Ct.
Canfield, OH 44406
Racing
http://www.teamglenwood.com/

Columbus Outdoor Pursuits
PO Box 14384
Columbus, OH 43214-0384
Touring Mtn
http://www.outdoor-pursuits.org/

Crawford County Cyclists
Barbara Dolch
840 Sunset Dr
Bucyrus, OH 44820-3155
Touring

Cres Cycling Club
Touring
http://www.pattymerry.com/ccc/

Cuyahoga Falls Mtn. Bike Team
Marc Stuhldreher
1764 10th St
Cuyahoga Falls, OH 44221
Cfmtbteam@aol.com

Dayton Cycling Club
PO Box 94
Dayton, OH 45409-0094
All
http://www.daytoncyclingclub.org/

Fairfield Schwinn Cycloids
4860 Dixie Hwy.
Fairfield, OH 45014-1911

Family Cycling Association
c/o Edward Stewart
PO Box 867
Elyria, OH 44036-0867
Touring
http://www.family-cycling.org/

Flatlanders Bicycle Club
PO Box 134
Fremont,, OH 43420-0134
Touring
Flatlandersbikeclub@yahoo.com
http://www.flatlanders.info/

Folks On Spokes
Douglas J Bower
1334 Concord St. NW
Massillon, OH 44646
Touring
http://www.geocities.com/
yosemite/7036
Folksonspokes@geocities.com

Franklin Bicycle Club
1050 Bernard Rd.
Columbus, OH 43221-1610

French City Cyclists
419 4th Ave.
Gallipolis, OH 45631-1110

Greater Ohio Tandem Society
(Goats)
10566 Stablehand Dr
Cincinnati, OH 45242
Touring
http://www.cinti.net/~gdbouit/goats.htm

Grand Lake Y Bicyclists
5511 Johnson Rd.
Celina, OH 45822-9003

Hancock Handlebars
PO Box 232
Findlay, OH 45839-0232
Touring
http://www.hancockhandlebars.org/

Heart Of Ohio Tailwinds
PO Box 176
Marion, OH 43301-0176
Touring Info@hot-tamale.org
http://www.hot-tamale.org/

Hocking Hills Bicycle Club
Earl Timberlake
11834 State Route 93 N
Logan, OH 43138-9313
Touring/mtn

Ksu Bicycle Club
191 Macc Anx
Kent, OH 44242-0001

Lake Effect Cycling
2958 College St
Austinburg, OH 44010
Lakeeffectcycling.com
Lakeeffectcycling@hotmail.com

Lake Erie Wheelers
PO Box 26146
Fairview Park, OH 44126-0146
Touring/racing
http://www.lakeeriewheelers.org/

Licking County Bicycle Club
PO Box 593
Newark, OH 43058-0593
Touring

Ohio Bicycle Clubs (continued)

Lima Council Hi-Ayh
PO Box 173
Lima, OH 45802-0173
Touring
Www.greaterlima.com/limaayh

Little Mountain Velo
Jim Behrens
355 S State St
Painesville, OH 44077

Lorain Wheelmen
PO Box 102
Amherst, OH 44001-0102
Touring
http://www.eriecoast.com/
~lorainwheelmen

Mad River Wheelmen
283 State Route 292 S
Zanesfield, OH 43360

Mahoning Valley Cycling Club
Alan Wenger
263 E Pine Lake Rd.
North Lima, OH 44452-9748
Racing

Major Taylor Bike Club
c/o George Harper
5623 Chowning Way
Columbus, OH 43213
Touring
Mtcc2000@insight.rr.com

Mantua Bike Club
Glenn Talmon
10939 Peck Rd.
Mantua, OH 44255-9211
Touring

Marietta Rowing & Cycling Club
PO Box 223
Marietta, OH 45750-0223

Maumee Valley Wheelmen
Sherry Simon
17 Kingsview St
Perrysburg, OH 43551-3107
Racing
http://www.freewheel.com/mvw/

Medina County Bicycle Club
PO Box 844
Medina, OH 44258-0844
Touring
http://www.medinabikeclub.org/

Mid Ohio Bikers
PO Box 844
Mansfield, OH 44901-0844
Touring
http://www.midohiobikers.org/

Mountain Mudders
38960 Staneart Rd.
Albany, OH 45710

Nationwide Bike Club
1 W Nationwide Blvd
Columbus, OH 43215-2220

Neobike
Kevin Kimmich
234 E King St
Chardon, OH 44024-1315
Racing
http://www.neobike.org/
Kevin_kimmich@simcom.net

Northeast Ohio Cycling Club Of Ashtabula
Dennis Steidaner
1013 Mill St
Conneaut, OH 44030

Northwest Cycling Club
1375 Inglis Ave.
Columbus, OH 43212-3557

Norwalk Bike Club
44 E Main St
Norwalk, OH 44857-1515
Touring

Oakley Cycle Club
3010 Madison Rd.
Cincinnati, OH 45209-1710

Ohio City Bicycle Co-op
3404 Lorain Ave.
Cleveland, OH 44113-3704
Bicycle Education
http://www.ohiocitycycles.org/

Ohio Randonneurs
1488 River Trail Dr
Grove City, OH 43123-9057
Endurance Touring
http://www.ohiorandonneurs.com/
Rba@ohiorand.org

Ohio Valley Bicycle Club
PO Box 63
Gallipolis, OH 45631
http://www.ohiovalleybicycleclub.
org/
Mtn

Ohio University Mtn Bike Club
Campus Rec Center
Athens, OH 45701
Mtn

Ohio Volkssport Association
721 S Detroit St
Xenia, OH 45385-5507
Touring

Ohio Wheeling Volksbikers
4842 Westmont Dr
Springfield, OH 45503-5836
Touring

Out-spokin Wheelmen
PO Box 838
Youngstown, OH 44501
Touring
http://www.cboss.com/osw

Orrville Cycling Club
9658 W High St
Orrville, OH 44667
Touring/racing/mtn
http://www.orrvillecycling.com/

Oxford Cycling Club
PO Box 774
Oxford, OH 45056-0774
Touring
Mcreech@fuse.net

PDQ Cleveland
348 Wyleswood Dr
Berea,, OH 44017
Racing
http://www.pdqcleveland.org/
Pdq_cleveland@yahoo.com

Premier Velo
104 W Union St
Athens, OH 45701-2751
Racing

Queen City Wheels
Doug Dobrozsi
9273 Kempergrove Ln
Loveland, OH 45140
Racing
http://www.qcw.org/
Ddobrozsi@cinci.rr.com

Road Soldiers Cycling Club
Ohio Veterans Home
3416 Columbus Ave.
Sandusky, OH 44870
Touring
http://www.roadsoldiers.com/

Seneca Sprockets Bike Club
PO Box 96
Tiffin, OH 44883
Touring
http://www.senecacounty.com/
sprockets

Shauck Area Cyclist
PO Box 161
Shauck, OH 43349-0161
Touring

Silver Wheels
PO Box 867
Elyria, OH 44036-0867
Touring
Www2.loraincounty.com/
silverwheels/

Society Velo
355 S State St
Painesville, OH 44077-3531

Spectrum Cycling Club
416 N Water St
Loudonville, OH 44842-1233

Spectrum Performance Club
1060 Reed St
Mansfield, OH 44906-1961

Spokes Bicycle Club
3944 Farmbrook Ln
Columbus, OH 43204

Ohio Bicycle Clubs (continued)

Square Wheels
Paul Salupante
3001 E Overlook Rd.
Cleveland, OH 44118-2437
Racing
Pfs@po.cwru.edu

St Charles Cycle Club
2010 E Broad St
Columbus, OH 43209-1665

Stark County Bicycle Club
PO Box 8863
Canton, OH 44711-8863
Touring/racing
http://www.bikescbc.com/
Bikescbc@bikescbc.com
Racing Team: http://www.starkvelo.com/

Summit Freewheelers
1191 W Sunsetview Dr
Akron, OH 44313
Racing   Egi@neo.rr.com
http://www.summitfreewheelers.com/

Tailwinds Bicycle Club
2323 W Bancroft St
Toledo, OH 43607-1306

Team Polkadot
Mike & Diane Clingerman
5315 Carina Court E
Hilliard, OH 43026
Touring
Web Site
Mclinger@columbus.rr.com

Toledo Area Bicyclists
1463 Craigwood Rd.
Toledo, OH 43612
Touring
http://www.tabnet.org/

Toledo Council Ayh-Hi
PO Box 352736
Toledo, OH 43635-2736
Touring
http://www.freewheel.com/hiayh/
index.htm

Tri State Wheelers
208 Beacon Dr
Weirton Wv 26062-4904

Union County Windbreakers
19901 Orchard Rd.
Marysville, OH 43040-9046

Vermilion Bicycle Club
14807 Mason Rd.
Vermilion, OH 44089-9230

Wandering Wheels Volkssports
501 N Market St
Shreve, OH 44676-9767
Touring

Western Reserve Wheelers
1422 Euclid Ave. Ste 1104
Cleveland, OH 44115-2063
Touring
http://www.westernreservewheelers.
com/

Westerville Bicycle Club
PO Box 356
Westerville, OH 43086-0356
Tour Race Mtn
http://www.westervillebicycleclub.
org/

Wilmington Bicycle Club
PO Box 94
Reesville, OH 45166
Touring
http://www.wilmingtonbicycleclub.
org/

WSU Wright Wriders
Wright State Univrsity # D09PE
Dayton, OH 45435

Wonders On Wheels
2203 Maryland Dr
Xenia, OH 45385

Trail Index

Trail Name	Page No.
Adena Recreation Trail	22
Alum Creek State Park	24
Barkcamp State Park	26
Beaver Creek State Park	28
Bedford Reservation	42
Big Creek Reservation	44
Bike and Hike Trail	30
Black River Reservation	164
Blackhand Gorge Bikeway	32
Brecksville Reservation	42
Buck Creek Trail	164
Buckeye Trail	34
Caesar Creek State Park	36
Celina to Coldwater Bike Trail	165
Cleveland Lakefront State Park	39
Cleveland Metroparks	42
Conotton Creek Trail	50
Creekside Trail	100
Dillon State Park	52
East Fork State Park	54
Euclid Creek Reservation	42
Findley State Park	56
Gallipolis Bike Path	58
Garfield Park Reservation	42
Great Miami River Recreation Trail	94
Great Ohio Lake to River Greenway	60
Great Seal State Park	66
Greenway Corridor Bikeway	165
Hamilton Bikeway	165
Harbin Park Mountain Bike Trail	68
Headwaters Trail	166
Heritage Rail-Trail	114
Hinckley Reservation	43
Hockhocking-Adena Bikeway	70

Trail Index (continued)

Trail Name	Page No.
Holmes County Trail	72
Hueston Woods State Park	74
Huntington Reservation	43
Huron River Greenway	76
I-480 Bikepath	166
Jefferson Lake State Park	78
John Bryan State Park	80
Kettering Recreation Trail	100
Kokosing Gap Trail	84
Lake Hope State Park	86
Lebanon Countryside Trail	88
Lester Trail	167
Licking County Recreation Trails	116
Little Beaver Creek Greenway Trail	62
Little Miami Scenic Trail	121
Lunken Airport Bike Path	167
Mad River Recreation Trail	100
Mary Jane Thurston State Park	90
Mill Creek Metroparks Bikeway	61
Mill Stream Run Reservation	45
Montgomery County Trails	92
National Road Bikeway	168
Nickelplate Trail	168
North Chagrin Reservation	46
North Coast Inland Trail	102
Oak Openings Preserve Metropark	106
Oakwood Park	169
Ohio & Erie Canal Reservation	47
Ohio & Erie Towpath Trail	110
Ohio to Erie Trail	108
Olentangy-Scioto Bikeway	125
Paint Creek State Park	130
Panhandle Trail	116
Pike State Forest	132

Trail Name	Page No.

Piqua Linear Park 169
Prairie Grass Trail 119
Richland B&O Trail 134
Rocky River Reservation 48
Scioto Trail State Forest & Park 136
Shaker Trail 138
Simon Kenton Trail 140
Sippo Valley Trail 142
Slippery Elm Trail 146
South Chagrin Reservation 43
Stavich Bicycle Trail 148
Stillwater River Recreation Trail 98
Stonelick State Park 150
Thomas J Evans Trail 116
University Parks Bike-Hike Trail 152
Van Buren State Park 154
Vulture's Knob 156
Wabash Cannonball Trail 158
West Branch State Park 160
Western Reserve Greenway 61
Westerville Bikeway 169
Wolf Creek Recreation Trail 96
Wright Brothers Bikeway 170
Zanes Bikeway 170

Surfaced Trails

Trail Name	Page No.
Adena Recreation Trail	22
Bedford Reservation	42
Big Creek Reservation	44
Bike and Hike Trail	30
Black River Reservation	164
Blackhand Gorge Bikeway	32
Brecksville Reservation	42
Buck Creek Trail	164
Celina to Coldwater Bike Trail	165
Cleveland Lakefront State Park	39
Cleveland Metroparks	42
Conotton Creek Trail	50
Creekside Trail	100
Euclid Creek Reservation	42
Gallipolis Bike Path	58
Garfield Park Reservation	42
Great Miami River Recreation Trail	94
Great Ohio Lake to River Greenway	60
Greenway Corridor Bikeway	165
Hamilton Bikeway	165
Headwaters Trail	166
Heritage Rail-Trail	114
Hinckley Reservation	43
Hockhocking-Adena Bikeway	70
Holmes County Trail	72
Huntington Reservation	43
Huron River Greenway	76
I-480 Bikepath	166
Kettering Recreation Trail	100
Kokosing Gap Trail	84
Lebanon Countryside Trail	88
Lester Trail	167
Licking County Recreation Trails	116
Little Beaver Creek Greenway Trail	62

Trail Name	Page No.
Little Miami Scenic Trail	121
Lunken Airport Bike Path	167
Mad River Recreation Trail	100
Mill Creek Metroparks Bikeway	61
Mill Stream Run Reservation	45
Montgomery County Trails	92
National Road Bikeway	168
Nickelplate Trail	168
North Chagrin Reservation	46
North Coast Inland Trail	102
Oak Openings Preserve Metropark	106
Ohio & Erie Canal Reservation	47
Ohio & Erie Towpath Trail	110
Ohio to Erie Trail	108
Olentangy-Scioto Bikeway	125
Panhandle Trail	116
Piqua Linear Park	169
Prairie Grass Trail	119
Richland B&O Trail	134
Rocky River Reservation	48
Shaker Trail	138
Simon Kenton Trail	140
Sippo·Valley Trail	142
Slippery Elm Trail	146
South Chagrin Reservation	43
Stavich Bicycle Trail	148
Stillwater River Recreation Trail	98
Thomas J Evans Trail	116
University Parks Bike-Hike Trail	152
Western Reserve Greenway	61
Westerville Bikeway	169
Wolf Creek Recreation Trail	96
Wright Brothers Bikeway	170
Zanes Bikeway	170

Mountain Bike Trails

Trail Name	Page No.
Barkcamp State Park	26
Beaver Creek State Park	28
Caesar Creek State Park	36
Dillon State Park	52
East Fork State Park	54
Findley State Park	56
Great Seal State Park	66
Harbin Park Mountain Bike Trail	68
Hueston Woods State Park	74
Jefferson Lake State Park	78
John Bryan State Park	80
Lake Hope State Park	86
Mary Jane Thurston State Park	90
Oakwood Park	169
Paint Creek State Park	130
Pike State Forest	132
Scioto Trail State Forest & Park	136
Stonelick State Park	150
Van Buren State Park	154
Vulture's Knob	156
West Branch State Park	160

City to Trail Index

City Name	Pop. Code	Trail Name
Many		Buckeye Trail
Akron	❺	Bike and Hike Trail
Akron	❺	Ohio to Erie Trail
Akron	❺	Ohio & Erie Towpath Trail
Alexandria	❶	Thomas J Evans Trail
Alta	❶	Richland B&O Trail
Amelia	❷	East Fork State Park
Ashtabula	❹	Western Reserve Greenway
Ashtabula	❹	Great Ohio Lake to River Greenway
Athens	❹	Lake Hope State Park
Athens	❹	Hockhocking-Adena Bikeway
Austinburg	❶	Great Ohio Lake to River Greenway
Austinburg	❶	Western Reserve Greenway
Bedford	❹	Big Creek Reservation
Bellville	❷	Richland B&O Trail
Belmont	❶	Barkcamp State Park
Bere	❶	Rocky River Reservation
Bethel	❷	East Fork State Park
Bidwell	❶	Gallipolis Bike Path
Bowerston	❶	Conotton Creek Trail
Bowling Green	❹	Slippery Elm Trail
Brinkhaven	❶	Holmes County Trail
Brookville	❷	Wolf Creek Recreation Trail
Butler	❶	Richland B&O Trail
Canal Fulton	❷	Ohio & Erie Towpath Trail
Canfield	❸	Mill Creek Metroparks Bikeway
Celina	❹	Celina to Coldwater Bike Trail
Champion Station	❹	Great Ohio Lake to River Greenway
Chillicothe	❹	Paint Creek State Park
Chillicothe	❹	Great Seal State Park
Chillicothe	❹	Pike State Forest
Chillicothe	❹	Scioto Trail State Forest & Park
Cincinnati	❺	Stonelick State Park
Cincinnati	❺	Ohio to Erie Trail
Cincinnati	❺	Lunken Airport Bike Path
Claylick	❶	Blackhand Gorge Bikeway
Cleveland	❺	Rocky River Reservation
Cleveland	❺	Huntington Reservation
Cleveland	❺	Bedford Reservation
Cleveland	❺	Big Creek Reservation
Cleveland	❺	South Chagrin Reservation
Cleveland	❺	Brecksville Reservation
Cleveland	❺	Mill Stream Run Reservation
Cleveland	❺	Ohio & Erie Canal Reservation
Cleveland	❺	Cleveland Metroparks
Cleveland	❺	Bike and Hike Trail
Cleveland	❺	Cleveland Lakefront State Park
Cleveland	❺	Ohio to Erie Trail
Cleveland	❺	Hinckley Reservation

City to Trail Index (continued)

City Name	Pop. Code	Trail Name
Cleveland	❺	Garfield Park Reservation
Cleveland	❺	North Chagrin Reservation
Cleveland	❺	Euclid Creek Reservation
Cleveland	❺	Ohio & Erie Towpath Trail
Clyde	❸	North Coast Inland Trail
Coldwater	❷	Celina to Coldwater Bike Trail
Columbus	❺	Olentangy-Scioto Bikeway
Columbus	❺	Alum Creek State Park
Columbus	❺	Ohio to Erie Trail
Conotton	❶	Conotton Creek Trail
Corwin	❶	Little Miami Scenic Trail
Coshocton	❹	Ohio to Erie Trail
Crosby	❶	Shaker Trail
Crystal Spring	❶	Ohio & Erie Towpath Trail
Dalton	❷	Sippo Valley Trail
Danville	❷	Kokosing Gap Trail
Dayton	❺	Stillwater River Recreation Trail
Dayton	❺	Mad River Recreation Trail
Dayton	❺	Great Miami River Recreation Trail
Dayton	❺	Montgomery County Trails
Dayton	❺	Wolf Creek Recreation Trail
Dayton	❺	Creekside Trail
East Liverpool	❹	Beaver Creek State Park
Elyria	❺	North Coast Inland Trail
Elyria	❺	Black River Reservation
Fairborn	❹	Wright Brothers Bikeway
Fairfield	❹	Harbin Park Mountain Bike Trail
Findley	❹	Van Buran State Park
Fredericksburg	❶	Holmes County Trail
Fremont	❹	North Coast Inland Trail
Gallipolis	❹	Gallipolis Bike Path
Gambier	❷	Kokosing Gap Trail
Garrettsville	❷	Adena Recreation Trail
Garrettsville	❷	Headwaters Trail
Glenmont	❶	Holmes County Trail
Hamilton	❺	Hamilton Bikeway
Hanover	❶	Licking County Recreation Trails
Hanover	❶	Panhandle Trail
Harrison	❸	Shaker Trail
Harveysburg	❶	Caesar Creek State Park
Hilliard	❹	Heritage Rail-Trail
Hillsboro	❸	Paint Creek State Park
Hiram	❷	Headwaters Trail
Homersville	❶	Holmes County Trail
Huron	❸	Huron River Greenway
Jewett	❶	Conotton Creek Trail
Johnstown	❷	Licking County Recreation Trails
Johnstown	❷	Thomas J Evans Trail
Kent	❹	Bike and Hike Trail

City Name	Pop. Code	Trail Name
Kerr	❶	Gallipolis Bike Path
Kettering	❺	Kettering Recreation Trail
Killbuck	❶	Holmes County Trail
Kipton	❶	North Coast Inland Trail
Lakewood	❺	Rocky River Reservation
Lebanon	❹	Lebanon Countryside Trail
Leetonia	❷	Little Beaver Creek Greenway Trail
Lester	❶	Lester Trail
Lexington	❷	Richland B&O Trail
Liberty Center	❷	Wabash Cannonball Trail
Lisbon	❷	Great Ohio Lake to River Greenway
Lisbon	❷	Little Beaver Creek Greenway Trail
Lockwood	❶	Great Ohio Lake to River Greenway
London	❸	Prairie Grass Trail
Lorain	❺	Black River Reservation
Louisville	❸	Nickelplate Trail
Loveland	❹	Little Miami Scenic Trail
Lowellville	❷	Stavich Bicycle Trail
Mansfield	❺	Richland B&O Trail
Mansfield	❺	Vulture's Knob
Mantua	❷	Adena Recreation Trail
Mantua	❷	Headwaters Trail
Mariemont	❷	Little Miami Scenic Trail
Marne	❶	Thomas J Evans Trail
Marquis	❶	Great Ohio Lake to River Greenway
Massillon	❹	Ohio to Erie Trail
Massillon	❹	Sippo Valley Trail
Massillon	❹	Ohio & Erie Towpath Trail
Medina	❹	Lester Trail
Milan	❷	Huron River Greenway
Milford	❸	Little Miami Scenic Trail
Millersburg	❷	Holmes County Trail
Mineral Ridge	❷	Great Ohio Lake to River Greenway
Monclova	❶	Wabash Cannonball Trail
Montpelier	❷	Wabash Cannonball Trail
Morrow	❷	Little Miami Scenic Trail
Mt. Vernon	❹	Kokosing Gap Trail
Nashport	❶	Dillon State Park
Navarre	❷	Ohio & Erie Towpath Trail
Nelsonville	❷	Hockhocking-Adena Bikeway
Nelsonville	❷	Lake Hope State Park
Nepolitan	❶	Oakwood Park
New Haven	❶	Shaker Trail
Newark	❺	Licking County Recreation Trails
Newark	❺	Thomas J Evans Trail
Newark	❺	Panhandle Trail
Newark	❺	Ohio to Erie Trail
Newton Falls	❸	West Branch State Park
North Baltimore	❷	Slippery Elm Trail

City to Trail Index (continued)

City Name	Pop. Code	Trail Name
North Olmsted	❹	I-480 Bikepath
Norwalk	❹	Huron River Greenway
Oregonia	❶	Little Miami Scenic Trail
Oxford	❹	Hueston Woods State Park
Painesville	❹	Greenway Corridor Bikeway
Piqua	❹	Piqua Linear Park
Rainsboro	❶	Paint Creek State Park
Ravenna	❶	West Branch State Park
Richmond	❶	Jefferson Lake State Park
Rockcreek	❷	Great Ohio Lake to River Greenway
Rome Station	❶	Great Ohio Lake to River Greenway
Scio	❶	Conotton Creek Trail
South Charleston	❷	Prairie Grass Trail
Spokane	❶	Great Ohio Lake to River Greenway
Spring Valley	❶	Little Miami Scenic Trail
Springfield	❺	Buck Creek Trail
Springfield	❺	Simon Kenton Trail
St. Clairsville	❸	National Road Bikeway
Steubenville	❹	Jefferson Lake State Park
Strongsville	❹	Big Creek Reservation
Struthers	❹	Stavich Bicycle Trail
Swanton	❷	Oak Openings Preserve Metropark
Texas	❶	Mary Jane Thurston State Park
Toboso	❶	Blackhand Gorge Bikeway
Toledo	❺	Oak Openings Preserve Metropark
Toledo	❺	Wabash Cannonball Trail
Toledo	❺	University Parks Bike-Hike Trail
Trotwood	❸	Wolf Creek Recreation Trail
Urbana	❹	Simon Kenton Trail
Verona	❶	Wolf Creek Recreation Trail
Waverly	❸	Scioto Trail State Forest & Park
Wellington	❷	Findley State Park
Westerville	❹	Westerville Bikeway
Westerville	❹	Little Miami Scenic Trail
Whitehouse	❷	Wabash Cannonball Trail
Wooster	❹	Vulture's Knob
Worthington	❹	Olentangy-Scioto Bikeway
Xenia	❹	Ohio to Erie Trail
Xenia	❹	Little Miami Scenic Trail
Xenia	❹	Creekside Trail
Xenia	❹	Prairie Grass Trail
Yellow Springs	❷	John Bryan State Park
Youngstown	❺	Stavich Bicycle Trail
Youngstown	❺	Beaver Creek State Park
Zanesville	❹	Zanes Bikeway
Zoarville	❶	Ohio & Erie Towpath Trail

County to Trail Index

County Name	Trail Name
(Many)	Buckeye Trail
(Many)	Ohio to Erie Trail
Ashtabula	Western Reserve Greenway
Ashtabula	Great Ohio Lake to River Greenway
Athens	Hockhocking-Adena Bikeway
Belmont	Barkcamp State Park
Belmont	National Road Bikeway
Butler	Harbin Park Mountain Bike Trail
Butler	Hamilton Bikeway
Butler	Little Miami Scenic Trail
Champaign	Simon Kenton Trail
Champaign	Little Miami Scenic Trail
Clark	Simon Kenton Trail
Clark	Buck Creek Trail
Clermont	Stonelick State Park
Clermont	East Fork State Park
Columbiana	Little Beaver Creek Greenway Trail
Columbiana	Great Ohio Lake to River Greenway
Columbiana	Beaver Creek State Park
Cuyahoga	Euclid Creek Reservation
Cuyahoga	Bike and Hike Trail
Cuyahoga	Ohio & Erie Towpath Trail
Cuyahoga	Mill Stream Run Reservation
Cuyahoga	I-480 Bikepath
Cuyahoga	Ohio & Erie Canal Reservation
Cuyahoga	Big Creek Reservation
Cuyahoga	Bedford Reservation
Cuyahoga	North Chagrin Reservation
Cuyahoga	Rocky River Reservation
Cuyahoga	Brecksville Reservation
Cuyahoga	South Chagrin Reservation
Cuyahoga	Huntington Reservation
Cuyahoga	Garfield Park Reservation
Cuyahoga	Cleveland Metroparks
Cuyahoga	Cleveland Lakefront State Park
Delaware	Alum Creek State Park
Erie	Huron River Greenway
Franklin	Westerville Bikeway
Franklin	Olentangy-Scioto Bikeway
Franklin	Heritage Rail-Trail

County to Trail Index (continued)

County Name	Trail Name
Fulton	Wabash Cannonball Trail
Gallia	Gallipolis Bike Path
Greene	Little Miami Scenic Trail
Greene	Prairie Grass Trail
Greene	Wright Brothers Bikeway
Greene	Creekside Trail
Greene	Mad River Recreation Trail
Greene	John Bryan State Park
Hamilton	Little Miami Scenic Trail
Hamilton	Lunken Airport Bike Path
Hamilton	Shaker Trail
Hancock	Van Buran State Park
Harrison	Conotton Creek Trail
Henry	Mary Jane Thurston State Park
Henry	Oakwood Park
Highland	Pike State Forest
Holmes	Holmes County Trail
Huron	Huron River Greenway
Jefferson	Jefferson Lake State Park
Knox	Kokosing Gap Trail
Lake	Greenway Corridor Bikeway
Licking	Thomas J Evans Trail
Licking	Blackhand Gorge Bikeway
Licking	Panhandle Trail
Licking	Licking County Recreation Trails
Lorain	Findley State Park
Lorain	Black River Reservation
Lucas	Oak Openings Preserve Metropark
Lucas	Wabash Cannonball Trail
Lucas	North Coast Inland Trail
Lucas	University Parks Bike-Hike Trail
Madison	Prairie Grass Trail
Mahoning	Great Ohio Lake to River Greenway
Mahoning	Mill Creek Metroparks Bikeway
Mahoning	Stavich Bicycle Trail
Medina	Hinckley Reservation
Medina	Lester Trail
Mercer	Celina to Coldwater Bike Trail
Miami	Piqua Linear Park
Montgomery	Great Miami River Recreation Trail

County Name	Trail Name
Montgomery	Montgomery County Trails
Montgomery	Wolf Creek Recreation Trail
Montgomery	Creekside Trail
Montgomery	Stillwater River Recreation Trail
Montgomery	Kettering Recreation Trail
Muskingum	Dillon State Park
Muskingum	Zanes Bikeway
Pike	Pike State Forest
Portage	Headwaters Trail
Portage	Bike and Hike Trail
Portage	West Branch State Park
Preble	Hueston Woods State Park
Richland	Richland B&O Trail
Ross	Paint Creek State Park
Ross	Adena Recreation Trail
Ross	Great Seal State Park
Ross	Scioto Trail State Forest & Park
Sandusky	North Coast Inland Trail
Stark	Ohio & Erie Towpath Trail
Stark	Nickelplate Trail
Stark	Sippo Valley Trail
Summit	Ohio & Erie Towpath Trail
Summit	Bike and Hike Trail
Trumbull	Great Ohio Lake to River Greenway
Vinton	Lake Hope State Park
Warren	Lebanon Countryside Trail
Warren	Caesar Creek State Park
Warren	Little Miami Scenic Trail
Wayne	Vulture's Knob
Williams	Wabash Cannonball Trail
Wood	Slippery Elm Trail

Find me a place, safe and serene,

away from the terror I see on the screen.

A place where my soul can find some peace,

away from the stress and the pressures released.

A corridor of green not far from my home

for fresh air and exercise, quiet will roam.

Summer has smells that tickle my nose

and fall has the leaves that crunch under my toes.

Beware, comes a person we pass in a while

with a wave and hello and a wide friendly smile.

Recreation trails are the place to be,

to find that safe haven of peace and serenity.

By Beverly Moore, Illinois Trails Conservancy

American Bike Trails

publishes and distributes
maps, books and guides for the bicyclist.

For more information:
www.abtrails.com